Landesmania!

*I dedicate this book to
those few who believed in and
encouraged me. And to
my daughter who will
read this one day.*

Landesmania!

PHILIP TREVENA

TIGER OF THE STRIPE · LONDON

First published in 2004 by
TIGER OF THE STRIPE
50 Albert Road
Richmond upon Thames
Surrey TW10 6DP
United Kindom

ISBN 1-904799-06-X

Typeset in the UK by
Tiger of the Stripe
Printed and bound by
Lightning Source
Milton Keynes UK & LaVergne, TN, USA

Who is Jay Landesman and does the 20th century owe him a favour?

Sitting at a corner table in the Groucho Club the man himself asked me that question.

Wearing a white linen suit (in the middle of winter), Panama hat and crooked grin, he was drinking a Grey Goose Martini and casting his eye over the shifting scene of humanity as it swayed round the bar, alert to a damsel in distress or a familiar face to exchange an impertinent quip with. Of the two there was never any doubt what provided him with the greatest buzz. The granddaughters of his first conquests were still not safe from that roaming eye.

As we talked, I felt that Jay was one of the last of the cultural interpreters of his time. A renaissance man of many parts and many parties, long before it became necessary to be a specialist to have your voice heard or a candy bar celebrity to be noticed. I liked the fact that he had a beguiling curiosity about people.

'Don't you dare call me an Ancient Mariner,' he said in his still broad St Louis drawl.

'He was that boring old loser that thought his life was a warning to the young.' His voice now took on the gentle, silky tone of the born showman:

'My life has been dedicated to the pursuit of its pleasures and an understanding of its mysteries. The young folk understand this and ain't finished yet.'

As that night ended I was impressed by the old bird and his cocky cheerfulness and was intrigued by what he must have been like as a young man.

And that is why on a cold night in the winter of 2003 I arrived at Duncan Terrace, in the northern reaches of London to visit the last player from the Beat days and check out the strength of his story...

I found the address I was looking for and pressed the doorbell. Nothing happened. I pressed it again just as a voice came over the door intercom. 'Who's that' it demanded in none too friendly a voice. It was a woman's voice. I was expecting a man's 'I'm looking for Jay' I started to say when she said 'don't ring my bell, he's down stairs'. Click. That was my first 'chat' with Fran Landesman.

I looked around for what downstairs could be and found a set of alarmingly steep iron stairs heading down to a basement flat I hadn't noticed on my way to the front door. I gingerly made my way down them and thought that with stairs like those an 84 year old was courting disaster, especially covered with snow as they were that night.

What the hell. I clumped down them with all the confidence I could muster till I found my way barred by an iron grill at the bottom. I knocked on the door on the other side of the grill and waited for the man to answer.

And then, there he was. Captain Grizzly himself. Jay Landesman. 'Well com' on in kid. What took you so long?'

The Panama hat was tilted over a bearded face and a generous nose that had a look of satisfaction about it. Dressed like a man who was getting ready for an evening Martini he welcomed me in.

I walked into Jay's den.

Aladdin and his lamp had decamped and left Jay to take over this grotto to memorabilia which one was either confused by or intrigued to ask questions about. Pictures that told stories and photos of a smile that never changed over 50 years. A clock frozen at 2.45 and a phrenology head wearing a pair of sunglasses to help keep its mute testaments to itself. Books and LPs and papers and other reminders of a curious mind. Decades represented by styles now forgotten and a sense that the dark brown, low lit den was home to a man and his lively memories. Eclectic and organic.

It was really one large room set up into areas for work, sleep, play, cooking, bathroom and a corridor that led out into the back garden. Just what a young boho would want for his 21st birthday. And just what an 84-year-old boho needed to hunker down to let the years pass painlessly.

There is something about a man no matter how far down his lifeline he has travelled that tells you how he used to be and the word for this man was dapper without exaggerations, stylish without affectations and cultured without falsifications. He was no mutton dressed as lamb.

'Hey Jay, looking good' was my natural reaction. He gave me a look and then in an impeccably growly 50s American voice offered me a martini.

I was going to enjoy this. This wasn't someone I was going to have to ask if I could smoke. Nor would a request for a second or third martini raise an eyebrow. As long as he had the makings.

We sat at a table groaning with papers and books and the things that can only find a home if there is only one table in the room and clinked glasses.

I had known this man in a glancing sort of way for about 20 years. I had come across him all those years ago, when his mistress at the time called it a day, and shortly after that, met me. United in our appreciation of this beauty.

But this was different. Suddenly we had clicked in this new century.

We had discovered that we had a lot in common. I was interested in his life and he was interested in my trying to tell it.

So now is the time to put on some lazy piano bar jazz, pour yourself a glass of what you like and keep the light low. Why don't you sit yourself in a comfortable sofa while you're at it and enjoy the story that's going to come your way. All you gotta do is keep turning the pages and think without envy of a life dedicated to the pursuit of a delicate pleasure.

I'll just hammer the keys to keep this barge afloat as well as I can and you just forget about me.

Benjamin Landesman: portrait of the artist as a young refugee.

'I do not know myself and God forbid that I should' (Goethe)

Martinis and women aside, Jay has never been one of the walking wounded who started life with questions about his relevance to the world around him.

Born into a time, 1919, just after the worst war the world had ever seen and arriving at his teens when America was in full Prohibition mode having exploded out of a decade of increasing debauchery it wasn't surprising that young Irving Ned Landesman, sensitive soul, was picking up some heavy vibes.

Briefly, because this is as interesting as watching a clumsy stripper's routine I'll tell you that he was born in St Louis, Missouri into a Jewish family that was hard to belong to I suppose but meaningless to you and me. And he had two brothers and a sister and probably a pet or two. Mother was the most important person of the family which is par for the course for Jewish families and his Dad was the silent memory as is the case so often. I can't tell you anything about the house or the neighbourhood or the flowers they grew because I just don't know. If you want to know, then go and read another book...

So I hear he was a nervous kid. Mother thought a psychiatrist could figure him out for her. Irving Ned obviously said what needed saying as he was returned to the bosom of his family in short order. You see what I mean about 'sensitive'.

He was the youngest 'sprog' of the family. We all know what that can do to you. Time to test yourself on the track set up before you. Daunting for some and a challenge for others.

His challenge was to change his no doubt lovingly given name and find a real name that would give him a life worth living... , and whatever the genesis, memory tells him that it was reading *The Great*

Gatsby. So at about the time most of us are dreaming of impossible heroes he reinvented himself as Jay. How wise that kid was. Tailor made to wake up the neighbourhood.

As he himself admits, his talents were never those of a boy who was going to work his way through the ABCs of spotty teenage angst but rather explore down the smart line and cheeky repertoire of the born hustler. Why stumble over your testosterone when you can dance around it and into the arms of money making schemes and the soft skin of girls not aroused by sporting jocks and stuttering nerds.

Remember that these were the Depression years. Unless you were a Champagne Baron of the old school most people were struggling and even if you were a kid there was an imperative to find a dollar or two through your own efforts.

Jay was good at this. Before he left high school he had already made a deal with his brother to sell him a stamp collection (after working at a stamp collector's shop and finding a way to pilfer a few) for a Ford T Coupé. Sounds good doesn't it? Except as it turns out the Ford was worth 28 dollars and the stamp collection 200 dollars. Still, it was the hustle that counted. But it would be the signature tune of his efforts over the years.

His parents ran an antique shop in St Louis but along the way his dad decided that he loved the style more than the profit that made his mother hum so he moved to Houston to find peace of mind and a life of appreciating beauty. Mother, called Cutie, for reasons that remain forgotten, continued the hustle with greater success.

I mention this only to show you that Jay was picking up the variations on a theme that would help him decide what side of the road he would choose in time. This pencil-slim example of louche youth was never going to make his home in academia for long. I would guess that a report card at the end of his high school years suggested Jay take his talents to the high street. Which is what he did.

As a matter of fact his talent for salvaging interesting artefacts from people's homes rivalled his ability to find interesting friends

Beatrice (Cutie) Landesman.

so he combined the two and set himself up with his own extension to the family business. The young man soon showed that his style was no passing fad but a natural extension of his sense of his own uniqueness.

Finding premises in a street known as Bed Bug Row he arranged his wares in the shop and laid himself out on a chaise-longue on his section of St Louis's weirdly wide sidewalks and watched the world go by with fascination.

Now this was 1940. Europe was already shivering in anticipation of the end of the civilised world while America was still debating the virtues of its isolation from that madness. And Jay? Well it's hard to say whether he was particularly concerned at all.

He was sure that no army would have him and no draft would get him. Good company and good jazz with well mixed martinis was the recipe he recommended.

His business came to a sweet conclusion at the end of that year when he put up his final sign in the shop for a favourite table lamp that was all he had left. Not For Sale. He could've been talking about his approach to life.

His War Years and his War Stories. Yes… well. If his father could've had anything to do with it this paragraph would've been loaded with action and engagement and patriotic fervour. I would've been shown a strip of campaign medals 58 years later and maybe had an 'aw shucks' story to tell you all. But the truth was, Mr Benjamin Landesman, German Jewish immigrant from the turn of the century, seriously patriotic American, couldn't get any of his sons into the armed forces. Every one of them rejected for various reasons.

Jay did end up briefly working for a war related industry. Though his work is still considered classified after all these years he felt it safe to tell me in this, the 21st century, and with most of the participants long dead and gone, that the main tool of his job was… a broom.

It would seem that, as the war got increasingly more serious and serious people were needed to engage themselves wholeheartedly with it, his services became less indispensable. Until it became clear to all concerned that his real role in life was to be back in the family bosom finding and selling beautiful antiques to help raise the spirits of the ladies left behind who needed therapeutic shopping and gentle reassurance to get through the grim war years.

And it was in these years that the family fortunes prospered as they discovered a niche market in finely cut glass, especially chandeliers, that would eventually lay the foundations for a fabulous enterprise. But that, dear reader, is for your tomorrow's perusal.

One of the consequences of the war years, and I know this is a long list but I bet you hadn't thought of this one, was that it reduced the supply of interesting people who were available for a good time. This was the worst sort of rationing for Jay.

St Louis was not overly endowed with lovable scamps and intriguing scoundrels in the first place but it had become a chore to find the right company to share martinis and social theorising with. So he headed up to New York's Greenwich Village, ostensibly to track down artifacts for the business but really of course to find some like-minded eccentric gamers. It wasn't surprising that he found them and even less surprising that he evolved a lifestyle that for a young man was pure bliss. With money in his pocket, a brief to look for beautiful objects as a job of work, and a clear eye for the merry practitioners of the arts of pleasure and indulgence, a man will find what he wants. Jay was going through the undergraduate phase of his social education.

Now some might start tapping their fingers impatiently at this stage, thinking that this fella was just getting too much fun, without any of the consequences most of us would suffer if we tried to do the same. I mean, didn't he end up in a nasty scene with a recalcitrant dame or get half throttled by a drunken marine on leave with one clever quip too many or get cheated out of a deal... or for Christ's sake didn't he even get a dose of the clap and a bout of liver quivers ... apparently not.

He returned to St Louis and immersed himself with the hippest people available, who, like in many parts of the world, are on the 'other side of the river'. This was the black jazz and blues scene in East St Louis. Billie Holliday used him as a chauffeur once.

But the real story that roams through the dark streets of all tall tales is a slice of midnight moonlight that spills across a table illuminating a martini glass emptied by the thirsty imagination of a man sitting just in line to get hit by a look that says… Hey Kid ! Gotcha

Jay fell in love. A lady now remembered because her father was a singing master of ceremony at a strip club down Bourbon Street in New Orleans. She was sweet and sexy. He proposed the day the bomb dropped on Hiroshima.

So ended his War.

Jay before and after adopting a macrobiotic diet.

'I share no one's ideas. I have my own'
(Ivan Turgenev)

One of the wedding presents they received was a monstrous Cardinal Richelieu bed, courtesy of the Landesman Galleries. It was a medieval wooden fantasy with carved dwarves holding up a canopy and a mattress large enough to hold an audience in. It seemed unsafe. But then it was an apt metaphor for the way he viewed his marriage.

Jay was by now settling into a crowd of returning war vets with twisted issues, congenial neurotics and part time madmen who called themselves the New and Forgotten men. Remember that the social tags of today were still not operational at that time in the late 40s.

The daily dreams were being looked after with the standard issue music, booze and American-fried, French literature sessions, while war surplus nightmares were taken care of with small amounts of chemicals that had started making their wary appearance.

Jay was a generous host for those who knew where to find him but he needed a larger forum for his offerings This was found when he became part owner of an art gallery bar, along with an ex-paratrooper turned bohemian businessman with the splendid name of Radulovich. Little Bohemia had arrived in St Louis.

This was where the Establishment came to date with Sin and the outsiders would become the outriders for the barn-fed, showing them what they were missing. One doesn't know how many were permanently converted in these situations but in later years many would be mentioned in dispatches when a rebel was looking for a role model.

But this lifestyle wasn't easy to accommodate in an otherwise sedate marriage and while our man Jay was still having problems pinning down his raison d'être. He wasn't sure if the identity card he was carrying at the time was all the world should know about him. In fact it was a recurring theme when his calling card no longer amused him: Antique Searcher.

A magazine was what he saw himself starting. Stories were pouring out of the mouths of the neurotic, language was beginning to jive and poetry was the new social currency. Not the academic pieces and classical constructs popular at the time, but raging torrents of angry statements and sexual challenges that threatened to go down the plughole unless someone could tap into them and give them a bit of a nursing.

And so it came about that one day while practising his balancing act between being serious and not he came up with a title: *Neurotica*.

In no time it made its appearance on a business card. *Neurotica*. A Quarterly Journal. Jay Landesman Editor and Publisher

The title said it all. A magazine for and about neurotics written by neurotics.

This title was approved by a fellow traveller, the poet Richard Rubinstein who talked Jay's language and the two of them sat down to find the manifesto that would back up the neatly coined name. They were not the only ones who were getting to grips with the new fad for psychoanalysis and its influences in art and literature, but they wanted to lay out a vision which would capture the imagination of the New Man, circa 1948. After much late night muscular debate and picking of brains that weren't yet pickled, a gradual outline of the manifesto appeared. And here is what they said:

NEUROTICA is a literary explosion, defense and correlation of the problems and personalities that in our culture are defined as neurotic. It is said that if you tie a string of red cloth to a gull's leg its fellow gulls will peck it to pieces.

NEUROTICA wishes to draw an analogy between this observation and the plight of today's creative anxious man... who has been forced to live underground but who lights his darkness with the light of his art.

NEUROTICA will present in as non technical language as possible, the authoritative scientists' approach to all aspects of neuroticism.

Then came the hard work of cold calling the letter boxes of those who could be suitable candidates from the creative world. The bait was straightforward. They enclosed a list of titles that would catch their eye.

'The New Look is the Anxious Look'

'Psychiatrist – God or Demi-Tasse?'

'Parties - Pathological or Otherwise'

'All the Good Roles have been taken: The Plight of the Talented Untalented'

'American Sexual Imperialism'

'The Drive to be a Misfit and its Reward'

'Art as Catharsis: The Laxative Theory as an explanation for Value-less Art'

'Can you Slap your Mother? A Semantic Problem'

'Choosing a Psychiatrist with Care: The need of an agency for helping the individual make the appropriate selection'
'The Unique Mores of the Bar and Tavern Social Milieu'

That is just a selection to give the reader of the 21st century a flavour of what was cutting the edge off and opening the envelope of contention and subversiveness, in the dog days of the first half of the 20th century.

The eminent and the famous were intrigued but it was those who had less to lose who began sending in their manuscripts. But all requested subscriptions.

One eminent psychoanalyst doubted if any analysts would be interested in writing for the magazine 'as they are much too neurotic to be associated with anything so neurotic as *Neurotica*. Best of luck.'

But the response was such that by the time they had their first issue ready for publication Time magazine had included them in a review of the little magazine scene in March 1948. They quoted the first line of their lead article by Rudolph Friedman: 'Getting married is the best way of taking regular exercise.'

Jay had finally found the conduit for his take on the world. Little Bohemia in St Louis had defiantly opened a window into the wider world of social anxiety and artistic angst, and his voice was beginning to be heard distinct from the herd

But one thing has never changed about America; which is that you have got to make the grade in New York if your ideas are going to wake up the nation.

'Ordinariness is contagious. Avoid it like the plague' (Samuel Pepys)

So it came to pass that Jay got on the 20th Century Limited and choo-chooed his way to his date with fate, dressed in black wearing a magnificent hand painted yellow tie and desert boots.

When you remember the way people dressed in those days with their standard issue suits and regulation hats then this man was looking like a vision of the future most of society would never see. It isn't something you get paid for and it helps if you are born with the flair but that don't mean it doesn't take guts to take the stares and snickers of the terminally grey.

He found a dime-sized apartment for two cents in the heart of the Village and started checking out his contacts for more contributors. Promotion of the second issue of *Neurotica* was essential. The baby needed the oxygen of publicity and Jay was preparing to give his lungs a good workout. The first to be contacted was a fellow who had contributed a short story to the second issue written in a little known vernacular that would later be identified as hipster speak.

That was John Clellon Holmes. Not having met him before he expected a sallow and strung-out midnighter... but instead found himself taken by a tall, amiable and shy professorial type. This was to be a theme in his time: there wasn't always a creative fire where you found the smoke and not all smoking guns were evidence of sharp shooting. Carnival mirrors prevented most of the social challengers from easy recognition.

But the next phantom that would be made flesh was a guy mentioned to Jay as unprintable. That made his day. A quick phone call established that he had a wonderfully weird name and the personality of a sociopath. Perfect.

John Clellon Holmes, Fran, Jay, Shirley Holmes, Knight
Landesman.

And thus he met G. Legman. Angry man extraordinaire with a
savage message against censorship and social and sexual repression.
The fact that the man looked like a wild boar on heat and lived like
one was neither here nor there. His life was as untamed as his intel-
lect was passionate, compelling and incisive. His thesis was clear.
Sex had been taken over by violence and he had the evidence to
back it up from comic books dating back to the 30s to the collected
thoughts of a hundred voices... including his own.

That first evening with Legman and a crowd of curiosity seekers
Jay had brought for protection would give him one of the main an-
archic thrusts to *Neurotica*. He would take Legman's manuscript
'Love and Death: A study in censorship', rejected out of hand by
every living publisher and make it a prophecy of the world to
come.

Clellon Holmes thought that they were made for each other. Legman and Landesman. A certain poetic symmetry, Jay thought. Madness was the verdict of his wife (oh yes, he was still a married man, though maybe only just) and assorted cohorts that were only sipping at the cocktail of events. It was a typical hot and muggy summer in New York in that year of 1948. Spanish Harlem was a sizzling place to go for a party in a crumbling brownstone with the sound of heavy bop coming from the top floor. Jay and company headed up the stairs.

A young guy dressed in an early James Dean look headed down past them to reload on beer. His name sounded like a whip crack. At the door a pair of apparitions dressed in bathrobes let them in. One of the them, a stick insect with a strangely large head giggled and fell on his knees before him in mock worship.

Identification was not forthcoming but more important matters needed attending to. Like what was the story of the scene and who had something to say. The people all seemed younger than him, dressed down in waterfront style and with the urgent repartee of the unpublished and undiscovered waiting for a man with the vision to see their potential.

Jay left the party later that morning sure that Legman would have blown them all away and that they were all kids who lacked the killer touch to get into *Neurotica*. Two names though seemed to be given a bit of extra respect by their peers. Whipcrack turned out to be Kerouac and the Giggler was Ginsberg.

There would be other parties. Many of them. But some of them would be dangerous places for a Jay to land in. All the established literature magazines, manned and womanned by academic heavyweights, exquisite dilettantes and flabby theorists failed to see the point of *Neurotica*. More than that, felt so uneasy about its intentions that they unwittingly sounded like just the sort of morning chorus Jay was gunning for.

But that only spurred him to make sure his distributor was getting his baby to the people who mattered: the alternative thinkers and antisocial youths out in the coffee shops, college bookstores and

G. Legman (photo Wayland Hand), former Associate Editor
and main contibutor to *Neurotica*. His articles included 'The
Psychopathology of the Comics', 'The Anatomy of the Murder-
Mystery' and 'The Rationale of the Dirty Joke'. He was expelled
from America for fighting censorship and fled to the French
Riviera where he lived until his death in 1999

corner delis. And all those who could hear the voices of change in
their head. The galloping neurotics with a magazine just for them.

The time came for him to head back to St Louis and go through
the motions at the Landesman Galleries and make up the financial deficit of his publishing endeavours. Before leaving he agreed to
have Legman partnering him in New York and looking for the edgy
writing he believed in.

The return to St Louis was not without its perils. After the buzz
and success of New York and the energy of its acolytes Jay had to

settle down to the business of doing business. From literary contender to antique dealer was a demanding shift in perspective, not
withstanding the all consuming paraphernalia and management the
magazine needed..

In the autumn of 1949 *Neurotica* came out in a new and improved format with 32 of its 64 pages dedicated to Legman's 'The
Psychopathology of the Comics', with a style of investigative journalism that would only become popular many years later. Lawrence
Durrell, Kenneth Patchen, Judith Malena and Holmes contributed
pieces that set the tone for exploring the psychological implications
of popular culture and its effect on the mainstream of society. The
established media grudgingly had to accept that it had a voice and it
had a vision. Jay Landesman. Publisher and Editor.

Much to his surprise he found himself praised from the heart of
the establishment. The critic Russell Lynes, of *Harpers Magazine*,
had stratified the American cultural scene into three categories:
Highbrow, Lowbrow and Middlebrow...putting *Neurotica* psychoti-
cally in as Highbrow.

This was a debut as stunning as it was unexpected. Of course sharing this pleasure with Legman was like trying to make his mother
happy. Not possible. Legman was sure that this was a ploy by the
intellectuals to take the fire out of *Neurotica*'s belly and warned him
that he had a new writer named Marshall McLuhan who was going
to savage the Luce empire. Jay's pride was tempered but not dented.
His partner, after all, was on his side. A true neurotic.

His opinion of himself, having once risen,
remained at "set fair" ' (Arnold Bennett)

Jay was ready to put his social themes into practical operation. Remembering that this was 1949, when words and deeds in relationships rarely matched and the vast majority of unhappy partners just got on with the business of bitching and surviving with alcohol and despair, Jay's intention to get a divorce and move on was radically single minded.

But it was time to get back to his real' baby' and get a grip on its baby-sitting editor in New York, one G. Legman, who was becoming a little too possessive of this weird child. *Neurotica* needed Jay.

Mission accomplished in St Louis and with the blessings of the patrons of Little Bohemia he boarded the train and headed for New York.

Jay didn't immediately hit the town in search of action. He was trying to figure out just what he wanted from the toy he had created. Legman was all for turning *Neurotica* into a torch. They both wanted light. Jay as in a light fandango pleasure cruise. Legman as in burn baby burn.

Remember Legman? Portrait of the angry man with a grudge against all those who had put his head in the toilet for being too clever and suspicious, but now with a weapon to use against the sexual conspiracy he saw all around him.

Jay knew that Legman saw himself as a Goliath in a world of thieves and perverts but he wasn't sure the battle was worth waging unless there was some serious fun to be had out of it. Sex did have its up side too, he reminded himself.

Jay linked back up with John Clellon Holmes who had become an established observer of the scene and looking much more a part

[21]

of it now. His home was the one of the refuelling stations for some of the more acute observers of the city beat.

The Greenwich Village bars were humming with a new code of behaviour which Jay had already noted in the piece he published, 'The Unique Mores of the Bar and Tavern Social Milieu,' which encouraged sexual adventure.

It was the sly eyes and the crooked smiles that gave him a thrill. The ones whose lives had the sort of juice that made Jay start the day in bed, kick off the evening with martini-inspired introductions and end the night with mambo-fuelled seductions.

Home for Jay became an apartment he rented on 53d Street appropriately between the Museum of Modern Art and Birdland. The new style had to be set up right. The streets were awash with stimulating incident as long as one didn't get up early for work, spend time in offices and then get home to a spaghetti dinner by the radio. And if the street aficionados had any talent one would find them in the clubs and cellars that were beginning to make an appearance for the soul merchants.

Neurotica was a magnet for them and, as the pilot, Jay was always the man to talk to. He was now full of restless energy, tossing out invitations to give him the story, finding the pulse of the city, checking out discarded ideas or inspiring people to shape a new one for him. Things had to flow and no idea could stand in the way of another coming up behind... get going and keep the door open behind you.

It helped that Jay didn't take himself too seriously. He saw himself as an enlightened jester rather than a wide-eyed revolutionary. He was ready to get people to accept their uniqueness rather than save their souls and if it could be done with a laugh so much the better. The New York diet of slang and pastrami was just up his alley. Jay had a good eye for the stories that pulled the zeitgeist out of that comfortable society and gave the chuckle to the serious observers of 'cultural analysis'. With his seersucker suit at the ready and his nose for an irreverent take he was tailoring the role of a non conforming cultural conduit.

But every Mutt has his Jeff... and in this case Landesman had his Legman. The counterpoint to Jay's insistence that life was a party and every story a celebration of it was Legman who saw life in his time as a thing born of mad violence and sexual chicanery. Moreover it wasn't recognised by the majority of its denizens because there was a conspiracy of constipated silence by the high and mighty which he was going to break with great wind.

A provocative partnership made in the full awareness that in time one of them would have to get the upper hand. It was too volatile to go hand in hand for long.

Then a bolt from the blue. He got a call from a friend working at *Time* magazine called Beka. Great name. She had been the one to introduce him to Legman. Strangely, because Jay thought of her as a lovely wild redhaired lady of good taste, she had once had a love affair with the man. But that wasn't what they talked about. She had what could only be described as extraordinary news.

In the strictest confidence she was telling him that her Boss, Mr Henry Luce, magazine publisher supreme was interested in buying *Neurotica* for his stable of magazines which included the world famous *Life, Time* and *Harper's Review.*

Small talk just faded away at that point. This was a moment to savour for Jay. Anyway you cut this it looked like it spelt success with a big mother of an S.

Beka then reminded him of why it was too early yet to savour this. 'Didn't I tell you Legman was just right for you?' Jay thought she was kidding. Apparently not. 'He's ruining, my life,' was his reply and he meant it

'Try having a love affair with him' she laughed.

'What do you think I'm doing?' shot back Jay.

Beka's parting shot was a warning: 'This is only the beginning. That man is devastating'

When he put down the phone it was with a mixture of panic and delight. If he had had a psychiatrist he would've called him... if he had had a moustache he would've twirled the damn thing into the night.

But what he did have was the sure instinct that this would have to be kept a secret from Legman till the time was right to bait him.

For Jay this was an unexpectedly early date with purgatory. On the one hand the vision of serious legitimacy, social calendar loaded with canapes and credibility, the opportunity to spread the word on a huge grapevine… and the money it would bring; on the other, having to deal with Legman and his unrelenting spleen and paranoia about just that sort of person, that sort of deal and the suspicion that Jay was a disgusting dilettante after all.

Why was *Neurotica* desirable for a man like Henry Luce?

Long before the days of confessional journalism and poetry and songs that were wrung out of personal experience, *Neurotica* had predicated the notion that the gap between the public and private life was both unreal and unhealthy particularly in matters of sexual hypocrisy. Maybe the links between pornography and violence attracted Luce's attention. This was a novel connection still largely unexplored.

The magazine was carrying such a combustible cargo that it was not surprising that at times it would burst into prophecy of cultural phenomena which no one else was even close to sensing much less describing. It had become a vehicle for all those who had a crooked tale and a twisted vision to share that was worth publishing and even though there were weird voices too, the majority spoke not only to their time but would also last the test of time.

For some of the more established voices it was a place to let out some of their wilder imaginings while for others it was the only forum open for their line of thought. For the readers it was quite simply the oxygen that allowed them to breathe in the belly of the whale.

Luce wanted those voices.

'Never forget that only dead fish swim with the stream' (Malcolm Muggeridge)

That phone call had put another complexion on the lifestyle Jay was enjoying in New York. The pleasure principle in the city was simple... the higher up the tree you were, the tastier the fruits. Now he had to convince Legman not only not to cut down the tree but to climb it with him.

He knew that Legman thought their real purpose in life was to influence and challenge the opinion makers so his line of attack was going to be that in fact they had enticed the biggest fish in the lake and won him over. Henry Luce himself.

But first there was the potentially explosive 5th issue of *Neurotica* to take care of. Marshall McLuhan had sent in his long awaited article 'The Psychopathology of Time and Life' which was in no uncertain terms an attack on Henry Luce, his empire and his intentions. It was profoundly researched and a devastating critique.

This just wasn't the way to treat the high and mighty if you wanted to join them at the top table, even if it was just to amuse them.

As it so happened that wasn't all that was making Jay feel his weather vane was beginning to spin dangerously. One of the offbeat sections of this issue was a parody of the personal ads of the time, aimed at fetishists and fantasists, but in fact written by *Neurotica*'s very own staff. Letters had started arriving for them, which seemed to be an extension of the joke, but it had left Jay feeling that this could be trouble. Remember the times and remember that almost everything that could be labelled obscene was. And there were penalties to be paid.

Well, by the time the 5th edition was getting mounted, Legman had decided that these letters should be published and suitably analysed so as to expose the extent of perversion in society generally

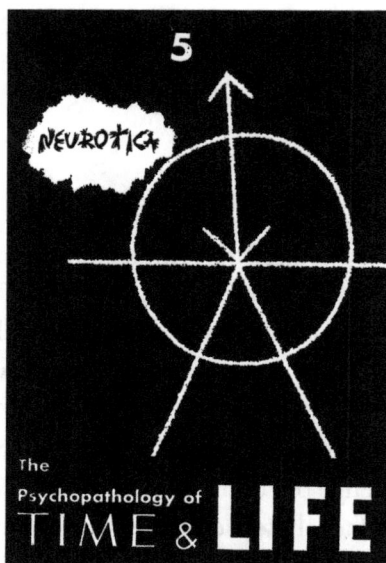

The infamous issue 5 of *Neurotica*.

and *Neurotica's* subscribers in particular. He had the title ready. 'Notes on Masochism'. The Post Office censors were going to have a field day.

With these thunderheads rolling ominously on the horizon the call from Luce's office was just the tonic Jay needed. A Mr Noel Busch wanted to meet. A meeting with the two of them and a perfect pitcher of martinis was Jay's idea of getting the deal done. But Mr Busch wanted to meet Legman. That was another picture because Legman insisted on them going to his house. That had little charm and no Martinis on offer. Jay tried to dissuade him but to no avail.

Busch was a sophisticated corporate type from Manhattan, accustomed to playing the gentile hatchet man with the desperately fawning who begged to be allowed to join the grand designs of the Luce empire. Going up to the Bronx to deal with a liverish Legman was something Jay tried to prepare him for knowing that Legman had agreed to the meeting with a curious cordiality that had made him nervous.

Jay probably could have written the script of how it turned out before it happened if he had been the sort to wake up from a nightmare with perfect recall. But Jay was a dreamer by day and by night.

Busch came from the school of carefully couched compliments and studious good manners. Legman did not. His school was the playground of insult and attack. Busch wanted to put Legman at ease. Legman wanted to embarrass Busch and make him feel like a village idiot. Along the way *Neurotica* became a fight between the Legman wanted to put Legman at ease. Legman wanted to embarrass Busch and make him feel like a village idiot. Along the way *Neurotica* became a fight between the Legman inheritance and the commercial possibilities of getting into the real world. The real world lost.

The evening ended when Busch finally drew down the blinds, and thanking Legman for his 'suggestions', allowed Jay to drive him back to civilisation in upper Manhattan.

Just to prove to Jay that this had had biblical echoes he was offered the requisite temptation. Would he consider going ahead with the deal without Legman? Jay's answer was fitting:

'It would be like producing Faust without the Devil'.

The reply was equally succinct: 'We have ways of making a magazine work'.

Somehow Jay had not managed to get his editor and high road partner to see the advantages of going into the lion's lair with full faith in their ability to carry the flag for their subscribers. In fact Legman made sure in the days that followed to remind Jay that he had been both unwise and thoughtless in pursuing the devil's road. They were making history on their own, and while it might be just a footnote when all was said and done, it would be a finer thing by far than simply being pinned to the mast head of an establishment crucifix for a season.

Jay took a shine to that thought... But how much does being a footnote of history pay? His mother could have told him but she wasn't being consulted by Jay anymore.

It all came down to that 5th issue of *Neurotica* which was now ready for printing. Jay reread the article by McLuhan. Maybe it was the time when he read it or maybe it was what he was drinking while he read it or just maybe there was another voice in his life that was helping him decide whether history or a serious cheque had greater appeal.

Many years later Jay Landesman would still be asking himself this question. A deep sigh would lead to a deep drink of his martini. And then he would talk about Fran.

Before that though, Jay had no illusions that by publishing that McLuhan firecracker, which was aimed right up the famously tight arse of Henry Luce he had signed away any chance of being considered a member of 'the meritocracy'.

But Legman had pressed the right buttons. Jay liked the dramatic moment more than most and if it came dressed for public spectacle so much the better. And this would be drama indeed for the America and especially New York of 1950.

There was a twist to the tale though. Remember the salacious letters that Legman had included in his article 'Notes on Masochism'? Well, those were a different sort of bombshell and the collateral damage would hit close to home. The expression' friendly fire hadn't been coined then of course (though had you mentioned it people would have thought you were emoting about your fireplace) but it certainly would have been clearly understood by Jay.

In those far-off days when policemen were respected, hats were worn by all men and cigarettes were healthy for you, the Post Office had powers to open any envelopes that carried magazines in them to make sure they were not breaking any of the many strict censorship rules prevalent at the time. Fetishist articles certainly qualified as naughty rule breaking.

Legman had convinced Jay that they could get them through if they went to suburban post offices to send out their magazine... and if they were examined and confiscated, so much the better because then they would have an enormously dramatic and public fight over censorship (which was Legman's whole raison d'être).

Jay by now must have been high on a martyr complex because he let this strident and righteous tone rule the day.

Not surprisingly as dramas go the Post Office did get into the act. One of the copies was opened, read by a scandalised postal clerk, confiscated and in due course Mr Landesman was asked to appear before the District Attorney of Connecticut. The upshot was that he could either make an out-of-court settlement or he could take the good fight to what ever lengths it needed to go. Legman was hopping with anticipation. Yes. Fight. Landesman was doubtful.

Finally it dawned on Jay that Legman should carry a health warning for anyone getting involved with him. Despite having sacrificed the Luce option, and having had to pay his way out of trouble, Legman was still berating Jay for not having the guts to take his fight against the censors all the way up the legal system. There wasn't a shadow of a doubt that Mr Busch would find this new issue of *Neurotica* as dangerous and offensive as a whore's tirade.

Legman's bone-deep conspiracy theories had now included Jay.

Jay's skin-deep interest in his sidekick's desire to create mayhem was coming to an end.

It was time to take *Neurotica* back.

After having his situation explained to him by a very expensive lawyer, Jay decided to take his advice and pay a hefty fine to make sure that criminal proceedings didn't take place against the good ship *Neurotica* and all who sailed on her. That of course incensed Legman, who despite having had such a good ally in Jay now denounced him as a pimp and impediment in the fight for the anti establishment cause.

One thing is supplying the weapon to a man who wants to fight a holy cause and another to be accused of not being a righteous enough standard bearer for that crusade.

Jay at the end of the day was not a crusader. Nor a preacher. He was Jay the mischief maker. Thank you very much.

So, reluctantly but ruthlessly, he decided that Legman was no longer a Landesman responsibility. It was time to take off those handcuffs and pay more attention to his own life.

'Is Sex Dirty? Only if it is done right' (Woody Allen)

It was time for Jay to fall in love.

He started looking at different material to include in *Neurotica*. Everybody he knew seemed bent on keeping a journal of the events and adventures that were making the buzz in the townhouses and attics, cellars and bars of New York. The energy being released was enormous and there was a whiff of dangerous fun every time a man and a woman got together who were prepared to remove the masks of conventional seduction.

Jay had been stripping down for awhile. He had never been an angel but his curiosity was now getting him into some interesting experiences with the ladies.

For those with a nose for the history of the tools of pleasure, I'd like to remind you of the existence at that time of the orgone box (an ozone energy field creator that stimulated the senses) and the manipulator which was a forerunner of the vibrator without the batteries.

But these would all prove to be the idle distractions of a man who was still waiting for cupid to string his bow.

On the anniversary of the death of Artaud an old friend of Jay's gave a party.

Naturally enough, as everybody there would be in turtlenecks and dark glasses, Jay opted for the suit and tie look. Perversity was at the man's core as we know.

But nonetheless he noticed a good looking girl, expensively square was his summation, that he thought would be a good tease. Pretty girls were his favourite canapé. Sitting beside her he prepared to take a conversational nibble but found that he was being accused of looking like he had just left the office.

'Oh yeah? Would you like a job then?' said Jay.

'I don't type' she said. And with that turned away from him.

Jesus, what did they put into THAT canapé he thought to himself. He found it easy to move away from her and not say another word.

But before he left the party he asked his hostess if she knew who that girl was. No, was the answer but with her knowing eyes she said, 'But she's your type'.

Jay muttered something about 'terrible girl' but he knew he'd like to see her again. Rejection often had that effect on Jay. Who needed a stimulator when a little rejection could be so intriguing?

Just a week later Jay and one of his pals, the celebrated writer and boulevardier, Anatole Broyard, were enjoying the first rays of the spring sun in Washington Square, when he heard Broyard say hello to someone in that velvety voice of his and continue with the introduction of his friend, Jay Landesman, 'editor of *Neurotica* and a very good mambo dancer'.

And there she was. The bitchy girl from the party but now with a smile that was warmer than the lovely afternoon. Jay knew then without a question that this story was going tor run and run. Apparently she thought the same. This was the first of many smiles that Jay and Fran would give each other over 53 years.

In the spring of 1950, like any spring really, what two young people needed was space to test the waters without interruption. The good friend was left high and dry.

Peaches was the name she had been introduced to him by and she looked just as soft and juicy as one. Her hair was golden, her teeth beautiful and for some reason he noted that she had a perfect gum line. Funny the things you remember when all is said and done and the sexual signals have switched you almost immediately onto the love track. Oh, and she had dirty finger nails. Desperately denying perfection.

Crossing the street as they left the park to go off and have that first drink together, a taxi almost ran them over as she prepared to walk nonchalantly across without looking. Jay managed to grab her just in time. Was it just to feel his arm around her or was her distracted air a fair indication of the protection the little lady was going to need?

While they sat at San Remo's and she drank Manhattans to his Martinis, he discovered she liked to talk about herself as much as he did about himself. This was going to be interesting.

For a start she definitely qualified for a scholarship to the New York School for Social Misfits. She was a promising Jewish Princess who had led her family a merry dance as she tried to find the right spin to the life she wanted to live. Needless to say, for those times, this involved dicing with the devil and being accused of weirdness that today would be thought of as normal and necessary. Peanut butter had been one friend (lots of it) and Greenwich Village would be where she would find others, some of whom in the nature of things she bedded. Along the way feeling that there was a romantic quality about the loser.

When she was 5 years old apparently she asked her mother, 'When am I going to get my freedom?' I can just imagine her mother leaping away, heading for the cocktail cabinet and telephoning one of her friends.

Jay could see that this girl couldn't be competed with in the rejection story stakes so he didn't try. But it was cocktail time and he suggested having one at his place.

As one does in the early evening there was a friend to visit in another bar along the way. A lady by the name of Bunny was the resident ivory tinkler and singer. As she sang her wistful 30s and 40s ballads Peaches confessed that she was familiar with them all, When Bunny came over to the table at the interval Jay asked her discreetly for her opinion of 'his gal'.
'She's just right for you', she said a bit tartly, as ex-lovers are prone to do.

Well, that was all right then. Everything was cocktail rosy. Except that for the third time in an hour Peaches had vanished to the toilet. But she returned soon enough.

Jay and Fran at a social event (photo Horst).

Just a short and now silent walk away was Jay's apartment. Once there she seemed less than impressed with his ad hoc style of decorating. For a girl that was now reluctantly going to a college of fashion and design this wasn't too surprising. But Jay wasn't about to let that indifference pass by without comment.

'You should've known me when I was in the antique business. This place would've looked like the set out of *Ben Hur*' he said, pointing to his satin eye mask and gilt mirrors as evidence. Despite that edgy intro to his domain, the artfully chosen music and the delicious martini went a long way to soothing matters. He even asked her for a dance as a man does when he knows every crack in his floor and every twist of his carpet so that there is no chance of anything but sublime gliding. But she insisted she didn't dance. Instead she made another trip to the toilet. It could've worried him but he was too infatuated to make anything an obstacle. Then she said

Don't think I'm crazy but could we go to my place. My folks are away in the country for the weekend and we can have it to ourselves'.

Well, why not.

Her parents lived in a fancy apartment on Central Park West which, not surprisingly, having heard how rich they were, looked like a small wing of the Metropolitan Museum. His antique dealer's eyes lit up at some of the items on display but mainly it seemed as if it had been done up in Good Taste 1928.

But importantly, the reason for her frequent toilet visits became apparent after her final visit almost as soon as she walked in through the door. Reappearing she said with a sigh of relief:

You're not going to believe this, but I haven't been able to piss since I met you. I was so nervous it was a misery'.

Not the stuff of immortal love songs perhaps but certainly a sign that there were serious feelings somewhere taking root.

Cue a nice cold martini sipped in a window seat overlooking Central Park watching New York twinkle. Cue a loving remark:

'When I was a kid I used to sit on the ledge of this window and look at all the little figures below me. Sometimes I wanted to join them with a big jump. I often think about death. Do you?'

That made Jay jump. And hug Fran (Peaches no more) like he had never hugged anyone before.

And then they somehow (you know how it is) found their way to the master bedroom and rather more joyfully did the only jumping that is worth the candle when you are swept up with a passion for someone... and life.

Sometime later that weekend, Fran's brother dropped round from his normal Village hangouts. Sammy the smart ass:

'Hey Franny, if you're going to let this guy meet the folks you'd better get him into the sun. He looks terrible.'

Jay knew he was in love when he didn't put the kid down with one of his honed killer quips, but smiled benignly instead. In fact he was composing a letter in his head at the time to his mother, to inform her that her crazy son had found someone as crazy as himself and was going to marry her.

Jay floated home shortly after.

On the following Monday there was a misunderstanding. These things happen. On Tuesday there was silence. Which is normal so you phone up even your toughest detractor for sympathy. On Wednesday Jay got a letter of apology from Fran. Ah, letters... Remember them? Swift phone call from Jay with invitation for dinner the next day. Accepted.

Thursday was the day for Jay to tell Fran what his story was all about. The antique business, the former marriage, the dominating mother, the identity crisis that had led to the creation of *Neurotica*, the problems with Legman, the failed opportunity with Henry Luce and why he wore a silk eye mask at night.

Fran couldn't have been more supportive.

'That crowd wouldn't have suited you. There is nobody hipper than the editor of *Neurotica*. I told my girlfriend about you and she was jealous.'

Jay was going to tell her about how he felt that he had failed to make *Neurotica* a strong enough voice against the savage repression of their society... but realised that one classy uptown broad in full rebellion was all he wanted at that moment. She was looking for someone to go down the dissenting path with her and he was determined to be that partner.

Sure enough, he was invited by Fran to come and spend a weekend in the country at her parent's house. This was a poor-little-rich-girl challenge to see if he was up to the mark.

He accepted. 'I'm looking forward to doing an inventory of your father's house.'

Which brought the immediate response in an old maid's voice: 'You don't by any chance love me for my father's Windsor chairs, do you?'

They were getting comfortable together.

The drive down to Connecticut wasn't particularly eventful but the setting was a perfect picture of the family. Chauffeur driving and cook beside him. Behind them, Fran's father in full millionaire self-absorption, her mother in silent chain-smoking mode... and Fran and the editor of *Neurotica* holding hands like forgotten kids. Big car.

There was only one way to deal with the situation Jay found himself in - with rebellion in his soul but love in his heart. He was going to get the attention of those dysfunctional parents by becoming the new house boy. So he helped to bring in the groceries, made a fire and mixed a pitcher of his excellent martinis. Then he allowed himself to be taken on a tour of the house saying the right thing on cue as if it was a play. Which it was.

But it became more like a movie when Fran took him out on the terrace where he could see the majesty of the forest around them and the beauty of the lake at the edge of the rolling lawn that ended in a gracious waterfall.

'Daddy's work,' was her nonchalant comment to his sigh of delight. 'He did it for himself, not for us.'

Even Jay thought that sounded a tad ungrateful but he reckoned there was time to work through it all.

That weekend was a mixture of bliss and blasphemy. There were sublime walks and flower picking, fantastic meals and sexy horseplay and of course Jay putting everyone at their ease with easy familiarity. But just being there reminded Fran of all the horrors of growing up as an unloved child in that idyllic setting which she couldn't help reminding Jay about. Alcohol in wholesale quantities had allowed the Deitschs (for that was her family name) to preserve a reasonable facade of a family not at war. Not surprisingly, Sunday was the day when guests came for lunch and it showed Jay how the attention her parents never gave Fran was used to full effect. It was easy to see why Fran was so resentful. Jay was getting the picture.

On his return back to his apartment Jay decided that it was time to set himself up a bit more comfortably. For Fran and for himself. Not a surprising consequence after spending a weekend in a millionaire's home, but then again, some people would wilt under that experience. Not Jay.

Their romance began to flower. Regular dinners in intimate French bistros, regular visits to art galleries, afternoon cinema visits to see old films, and museums galore. But Jay found that their tastes rarely seemed to coincide. For someone with such a rebellious streak about life her tastes in art seemed surprisingly square. But, in his sporting way, he decided to be her tutor in all matters of romance and literature.

Having spent so much time in the company of losers, it didn't surprise Jay that she was less than comfortable with his gang of friends, all of whom made their living and certainly their presence felt with wisecracks and long conversational rambles. But she was a good laugher, a talent all storytellers need to find in their audiences. Talk was the main activity; dead air was a hanging offence. She still wouldn't dance but she was game for anything else.

He also gradually started to introduce her to his family. On one train trip to meet his sister he made the discovery that she carried a little pill box.

She told him: 'I'm covered for any emergency: sugar substitute, aspirin, sleeping pill, pain killer, appetite depressant, Miltown – the usual equipment for a modern girl.'

Just the sort of comment that made Jay ever more protective of her.

By now they were spending regular weekends at the country estate where Jay had upgraded his status to court jester. All that fresh air was bringing out the happy kid in him, perhaps for the first time, but it also made him realise that he didn't want to lose this strange and insecure but beautiful babe. They were made for each other. As romantic as Zelda and Scott Fitzgerald and as cool, good looking and deeply shallow.

'I'd make you a damn good husband', was Jay's bid.

Fran countered with: 'Why don't I just move in with you?'

Jay surprised himself: 'None of your old fashioned immorality here. If you don't marry me you'll be sorry for the rest of your life.'

Enough said. Time to take the proposal to the upper chamber. Dinner with her parents at their house. Mother and daughter left the two men alone after the meal.

The TV was turned on. Jay courteously waited for a commercial break before saying: 'Fran and I want to get married.'

Once the commercial was over came the considered reply: 'How are you going to support her?'

Jay was on the ball: 'Don't worry about that angle. The Harvard University pay system has gone berserk and sends me cheques for subscription renewals every month.'

Then came the gracious reply he had been hoping for: 'I can't tell her what to do with her life. If you're what she wants, what can I say?'

It might have sounded a bit sniffy to a bystander but it was as good as a blessing to Jay's ears.

Jay chose his birth date as the day for the wedding. It was a few weeks away and in the midst of a typically muggy summer season so it made sense to have the ceremony in Connecticut.

There were mixed reactions to the new developments. Jay's friends were mainly impressed by how quickly he had wrapped up the romance though others were sad to see 'another good man go down the drain'. Legman, though no longer a partner, was still a presence of sorts and was only concerned that Jay should practice safe birth control: 'Take her temperature every day. In the rectum', he advised thoughtfully. Jay's mother, Cutie, was at last in on the act and like all Jewish mothers worked hard to get up to speed on what her son had done without consulting her. Her range of comments showed how this was happening. From:

'She's very unconventional isn't she?' as she met Fran.

'I hope I'll see you at the wedding,' as she said goodbye to Fran.

'I'm very happy for the both of you. You are perfectly matched,' as she gave Jay the eye before leaving.

Fran's parents were delighted to be doing something practical and made all the arrangements. It was a good wedding. The food was delicious. The champagne sparkled. The hired help were efficient. The flowers were beautiful. Everybody enjoyed themselves. Nobody forgot their lines and Jay's mother gave her wholehearted approval: 'You could've done worse'.

But strangely, Fran's father hadn't hired a photographer for the occasion, nor did he, a keen camera enthusiast, take any pictures. Let's be reminded that in 1950 very few people had a camera lying around for a quick snap or two. What that meant was there was not a single picture taken to remember the occasion by in years to come, nor was there a reminder for those who perhaps did not wish to remember.

Ah, and one other little thing. No honeymoon had been prepared.

Jay had planned to stay on at the estate luxuriating in splendour with his new bride but instead had found himself being discreetly reminded that tradition dictated otherwise.

The reluctance to leave was transparent in Jay and traumatic for Fran, despite the rice and well wishes thrown on their way. It was a dangerously quiet car trip back to a humid and stifling New York City.

Instead of starting out married life with an argument as so many fresh couples do, they said nothing to each other. For two rampant talkers this was punishment indeed.

Jay suspected that their perfect mismatch of backgrounds and pleasures disguised the fact that he needed someone in his life to give him a hard time. But while they may have both bought into the affair for the short term, they now had a long term view to figure out.

The silky Broyard, Jay's friend, invited them to spend the next couple of days on Fire Island with his girlfriend as his wedding present to them. The other presents they received were too joky to get interested in. Not Jay's idea of a serious investment. But then what did he expect? Gold plates and silver goblets encrusted with rubies? Well... yes, actually.

Each of them gradually forgave the other for having stepped on the other's shoes and started learning how to live together.

'The desires of the heart are as crooked as a corkscrew' (Auden)

Jay's flat was decorated in what a simpering interior designer would call Early Decadent. Everything was in black. A statement of the owner's penchant for the dramatic one might think, but a closer look would have told the limp-wristed connoisseur that here was one of fashion's early recyclers. As everything came with identity sores from various previous owners it was logical to give them new hope and a new life. Which Jay did.

But what gave the room its emotional impact was the hull of a wrecked ship that had been transformed into a piece of sculpture that hung on the wall. There were figures attached to the hull representing life at the bottom of the sea in Davy Jones' locker and a figure on the ship in the style of Giacometti peering through a telescope. An imperfect but not entirely inappropriate metaphor for Jay's adventures in New York.

In those first few months of marriage, Fran found herself hostess to an increasing flow of traffic in and out of the apartment. Most of it had to do with *Neurotica* business. Subscribers who wanted to meet their favourite editor and others who just wanted a chance to share the details of their sex lives with a man who cared. Because Jay reality did enjoy not only the doing of it but also the talking about it. Especially if there was a heavy frisson of fantasy attached to it.

Some heavy hitters also came to enliven proceedings with frantic bongo banging and scat singing from neon-lit afternoons through to early morning, stoned challenges to come out and play. Cassidy and Kerouac almost convinced him to dedicate a whole issue of *Neurotica* to Bop and its Brethren. But he fell asleep before saying yes. But he did agree to publish Ginsberg's new novelty poem. Easy come, easy go.

Strangest of all perhaps though was the night when Fran's parents decided to accept an invitation from Jay to come on over for dinner. This was a way to get them on his home ground and show how a beat and groovy guy lived. Why they accepted can only be imagined.

It was no surprise that it was more slapstick comedy than choreographed organisation.

Fran walked in with the groceries as they arrived. Nobody could find a comfortable place to sit as this time the floor wasn't an option. And while the father stood manfully waiting for things to resolve themselves, the mother swayed sorrowfully like an unhappy animal waiting to be shot. Fran was trying to cope with a kitchen that hadn't been cleared from the night before. And Jay. Jay had it all under control as he prepared a dynamite martini in his favourite herring jar while keeping up a brisk monologue describing the calendar events of the beat season.

Their next door neighbour appeared in piss-stained underwear asking for help to fix his toilet. As he was a pensioner Jay duly obliged. On his return the food was being dumped on the table by a grumpy Fran playing an irritable waitress scene. They sat down to eat.

'This isn't fit for human consumption,' was the growl that came from Father as plate and contents hit the floor.

Fran burst into tears.

Mother called her husband an animal.

'I'll drink to that,' seconded Jay, pleased that he had finally got his father-in-law's attention. As all of them had a high tolerance of psychic pain neither the ambulance nor the police services were required. It was just one of those nights.

Jay was becoming seriously attracted to the charms of country weekends at his in-laws. It allowed him to play the Country Gentleman in a play by an absurdist. His cast seemed willing to go along with the pretence that that was what the editor of *Neurotica*, his rebellious wife, the bridge-playing father-in-law and dipsy mother-in-law should do to preserve the illusion that there was an internal logic running this show.

Because let's not forget that Jay Landesman was first and foremost at this time of his life the publisher and now sole editor of *Neurotica.*

There was a society out there in need of a critical ravaging and writers had to be found to do it. Especially as Jay and Clellon Holmes did their thinking and research at a bar called Glennon's which collected all those who had fallen out of the limelight into the twilight of anonymity but still had by- god tales to tell. They would drink through a dozen good ideas and then a crowd of them would move across the street to P. J. Clarke's where the movers and shakers of Madison Avenue would congregate.

Flushed success drank with choleric failure cheek by jowl. The romantic losers let the pressure pack pay for the drinks of course. To make them feel better about their good fortune and remind them that what is given can also be whipped away. You don't say...

But on occasion Jay would stumble over a serious contender from the rich and untalented who wanted to be taken seriously as a writer. While a silent angel helping to bankroll the magazine might have been useful, a fat cat who wrote like a cheap canary was not only unwelcome but an embarrassment of the highest water.

Jay was getting a bit neurotic when he hit on the idea of writing an exposé of the creeping homosexual tendency that was beginning to make its appearance in the cultural arena. It was a well-reasoned article but his was a lonely voice that found no echo in those times though he would of course be right on the button in the years to come with his charge that the heterosexual male and his values were under threat. As a member of one minority, Jewish, he felt he was entitled to take a dig at another that was trying to undermine his manhood, which he took very seriously indeed. It appeared in *Neurotica* 6 under a pseudonym.

Legman predictably snarled at him: 'It's too big for you, Landesman. Leave that kind of thing to people who know how to handle it.'

[43]

It would be a long time before anybody else would and by that time we were living in a bipolar world.

*'If only God would give me some clear sign
that he exists - like making a large deposit in
my name in a Swiss bank' (Woody Allen)*

Jay, as I have said before, was not a crusader. A mischief maker certainly. But not a missionary either.

Neurotica was beginning to run out of laughs for him.

It was the spring of 1951. The 'Machine' issue of *Neurotica* had just been published. The gist of it was to develop a folklore of industrial man and highlight the role played by the machine in winning the battle against man instead of for him.

Marshall McLuhan was again a pivotal contributor, a man whose ideas were beginning to be listened to with increasing seriousness though few people knew that his idea of a good time was to go out with Jay to a restaurant with his own tin of sardines and then ask the maître d' for a pair of chopsticks to eat them with.

What with Legman's love of liver soup these two massive intellects obviously had something to learn about the pleasures of life à la Jay.

Things came to a head when on a bleak midwinter night a typically bullish call from Legman was made bleaker by his insistence that the 9th issue of *Neurotica* should be dedicated to the castration complex. Jay tried to sidetrack him out of that thinking but he might as well have tried to shift the angle of the Niagara Fails.

'You're morally bankrupt. You've sold out. You're cashing in on my ideas and all I get is a kick up the ass. You're going to try and silence me like all the other shitty editors I've worked with before. But I will publish the castration issue without you, Landesman.'

Jay let the rebuke settle then reminded Legman 'I published you when nobody would touch you. Think it over. Once you publish the castration issue, what do you do for an encore?'

He might as well have been talking to himself. In every sense of the word.

His enthusiasm for the full-frontal attacks of his erstwhile partner was wearing him down. The tag team doesn't really work when one member wants to chew off the opponent's testicles while the other is only interested in tweaking his nose.

Jay's country life dreams even took a whimsical bent as he envisaged himself taking over the barn in the in-laws' estate and transforming it into a country den for his city street players who like him were beginning to fray at the edges. Fran was about as interested in that idea as a nun in dirty sex. Which wasn't surprising, but when you're in escape mode you'll fly any idea up the mast just in case.

All his friends' relationships were flying apart at the seams. Husbands leaving wives and men ditching their girlfriends. It occurred to Jay that you couldn't stay married and make it in New York.

He wasn't even sure he had the audience he wanted for *Neurotica* any more. After sending out a questionnaire to his subscribers asking them for feedback on the magazine, he found that the response came from a constituency of terminally critical and evangelising perverts.

So Jay took stock of himself. Here was a man who prided himself on the cut of his cloth and who had bought himself a rare model Ford V-8 convertible to keep and drive in the country. He fancied himself as a possible writer in exile in Connecticut but the truth was that his freelance articles written with Holmes were being rejected. *Neurotica* was becoming a sideline and his main business was finding a way to live in New York without a cause.

Spring was in the air but it was just hanging there in the year 1951...

A surge of anti-intellectualism was washing through the streets. People were getting seriously flippant and dyspeptic as if they were preparing themselves for a role in a jittery and ironic show. Maybe it was the first shimmer of what would be called the cold war in later years but which at that time was possibly no more than a hint that with nuclear power on the horizon the red sunsets were not just drug and drink fuelled hallucinations.

Whatever it was, the overriding theme of the day was the futility rite.

Friends compared suicide techniques and parties took on sinister themes. The weak were bailing out and the strong were baring their teeth as though an invisible predator was stalking them. Perhaps the good folks that made up the *Neurotica* underworld were just not ready to be so high for so long.

Remember, you 21st-century alley cats, that 50 years ago this was all a new domain. This nervous set were just the scouting party to the pioneers of excess that would materialise in the 1960s. Social history would ebb and flow mightily between that cup and your lip.

As far as Jay was concerned the dream was over. The 8th and penultimate issue, the 'Machine' *Neurotica*, was published that spring. He had identified what he wanted to castigate in society and had done so. He had chronicled America's illnesses long before others had even recognised it and had amused himself immensely while doing so. It was now up to another breed of publisher and writer to take up the baton.

In the end it hadn't been a long run, more like a ten yard spurt... but as anyone with the slightest understanding of this sporting metaphor realises, those are often the hardest and the cruelest.

Jay decided to give Legman the magazine. Lock, stock and loaded.

Easier said than done of course. Legman came from a long tradition of looking a gift horse in the mouth and questioning the parentage of both beast and bone headed giver. Jay's argument that he was tired of trying to change the world and was now going to do a bit of changing of himself struck the eternally leery Legman as whimsical and foolish. But in the end he accepted.

The man still had a castration story or two to tell up his sleeve...

But the real reason for the dramatic decision was that Jay and Fran weren't having fun any more.

Jay had gone to visit his older brother Fred (happily married to the lovely Paula) who had rented a house in Connecticut for the summer, and had compared their comfortable family bonding with his and Fran's madcap gallivanting around New York. It dawned on him that he hadn't taken his own marriage seriously enough and it was in danger of falling into the neurotic abyss that he had helped encourage

It was time to reinvent himself as a husband and return to the business world. It was time to return to St Louis.

Fran was entirely ecstatic at this turn of events. Not. This was a big city girl being asked to up sticks and head for a provincial purgatory. Jay suggested that if she grew to hate it she could always return to her mother and father. That made her think. It was dirty pool but it worked. He made it easier for her by quoting Elsa Maxwell's farewell to New York that had just been published in Ed Sullivan's column:

'I'm so sad to leave my favourite jungle, New York. Lawless, careless, casual, terrible, electric, thrilling, murderous, heartbreaking, gay, fascinating, divine New York.'

Most of those adjectives had been filed by the pair of them, though nervous would have replaced murderous in their lexicon of experience.

The farewell party reminded Jay of those he had gone to when he first arrived. But instead of looking for a way in he was now the host on his way out. But the beautiful and wasted, limelighters and candle holders who came to get the last of the Landesman hospitality were no longer the voices that inspired him. Some of course would go on to achieve various degrees of fame but at the time they all seemed as if they had made a losing pact with the devil.

They left on an evening, in Jay's touring car, the summer sun setting among the towers, while the canyon streets were filling up in the lengthening shadows with the raucous cries of the peddlers of New York fiction.

'Take care to get what you like or you will be forced to like what you get' (G. B. Shaw)

It was a seamless transition for Jay. The voice of the Beat Generation was now a fun loving businessman.

He had been ready to become part of the Landesman Galleries for awhile.

Fran on the other hand was a lime trying to grow in an orange grove.

It wasn't a problem of people not wanting to entertain this sophisticate but rather that the lady had little to do while Jay enjoyed his notoriety in an entirely appropriate way for a man of his time. I would imagine the men were a bit too predictably loud for her while the women just purred with Jay around.

Brother Fred was a man of quiet genius. Always thinking up new projects for the Landesman Galleries he was also a man who wanted people to have a good time. And he understood the value of giving people what they needed in a place where he could control the takings. Business and pleasure were like vodka and vermouth to him. Here was a man who had mastered the real meaning of a Perfect Martini.

So it was no surprise that one day he said to Jay: 'Look, we could use a place to hang out in. Attract some new faces. Have a party. Let's treat ourselves to a bar. Even if it closes in a month, it won't cost us much.'

Jay must been having one of his serious days. So Fred pushed the fun button:

'There's nowhere decent to have a drink in this town. What do you think?'

All Jay had been thinking about was that this proposition was delightful. But not entirely a marriage building suggestion.

Fred wasn't finished: 'It would be something for Fran to do. She could decorate the place; she has a good eye for that sort of thing.'

Jay was still thinking. But that ain't the road to motherhood, was, would you believe it, what he was thinking...

Until a few months after New Year when Fred asked him to look at a place that had just come on the market.

'It's the old queer bar, Dante's Inferno, that's been closed since New Year's Eve. It's got such a reputation that it's going for a song.'

Fred could never resist a bargain. Jay couldn't resist a challenge to his sense of fun.

They visited the joint and found a bar with a tiny stage, cluttered with the leftovers of its last and closing night. It looked sad and tacky to the uncultured eye but the brothers Landesman saw its potential. Fred bought it that same afternoon.

Fran was offered the job of designing this new project. Fred smiled wickedly:

'There's just one thing. Don't count on me to do any work but I'll give you anything you need to make into the place you want.'

For the next month Fred worked full time as the line producer of the project, consulting with Fran every step of the way, while friends worked on gutting and stripping the place down for its makeover. Out went the Formica, in went the marble. Out went the neon lighting and in came the chandeliers (hey reader, remember those. Mentioned them at the start of the book. Look lively now). The brick walls were painted black. The bar top was given a facial that left it looking reborn. But the most important aspects of the bar's new personality were coming out of Fred's back rooms at the antique galleries, as if waiting all this time for this moment: drug store chairs, doors of etched glass, elevator grills, marble busts, gold leaf pier mirrors, brass monkeys and a huge mirror, so seductive and eye catching that even if you weren't narcissistic before you gazed in it you would certainly be before you could tear your eyes away from your suddenly theatrical poses. All barflies know the power of the mirror.

The Crystal Palace: Out went the Formica, in went the marble.
Out went the neon lighting, in went the chandeliers. The bar top
was stripped of a thousand rings. Jay and Fran used many things
– drug store chairs, doors of etched glass, elevator grills, marble
busts, gold leaf pier mirrors. Above the bar went a miror so
seductive it made ugly people look handsome.

I remind you all to remember that what we see today up and down the streets whose only raison d'être is to provide the setting for distinctive watering holes, was once upon a time bars that were there simply to give you a drink, a spittoon, some sawdust on the floor and a couple of options of where to piss...

So many Landesman chandeliers were used that such a shower of crystal would inevitably lead to this pasha's suite of a bar being officially christened The Crystal Palace.

Jay's role in all of this was inevitably to make sure it had some sort of organisation. The right person had to be hired to give the palace the tone and style it deserved. Preferably with the talent to amuse and be different. And with multiple personalities would help, as Jay had in mind a manager who could double as a bartender, accountant, bouncer and sociologist. Fran had just the guy. A taxi driver, collector of *Neurotica* and, just as importantly, a friend of hers, with the splendid name of Shepard Rifkin.

A bartender was next. Of course he had to be able to mix the cocktails and pour the drinks. But could he be provocative and seductive while he was doing the basics and yet look like a bruiser with a degree in political unrest if called upon?

An Irishman by the name of Jack O'Neil fitted the bill. He was Jay's inspired first and only interview.

Jay was fully engaged now in running the Galleries so he only had time to come in to the Palace in the evenings when he would take up post behind the bar and make his Martinis till the crowd got interesting and loud, and the workload too serious. But he also realised that there could only be one star bartender operating at a time and O'Neil was proving to be that attraction. Ruthless with those who didn't respect his rules and games, reassuring to those who were not quite up to speed, reprimander supreme if someone was losing the script and heavyweight remover if they had lost the plot.

This was a bar that unofficially was a gentleman's club to encourage the art of drinking and keep the bartender savant amused. Ladies were encouraged to keep the gentlemen coming but not necessarily to hang around themselves. This was the cocktail hour for men and their brand of gossiping and tearing a strip off their working day. Women, one has to remember, were not yet sharing power games at the office.

So what was Jay up to then?

News from New York had reinforced his sense that he had left the place at the right time. Legman had lost his case against the censors and had fled to Paris. From there he sent Jay a letter asking him to send him guilt money because 'my wife is sick and I am going blind'. Jay did. His fellow conspirators, Clellon Holmes and Anatole Broyard, had recently brought books out detailing the scene in the New York they had all shared. But somehow Jay felt that it wasn't exactly what he had experienced and was getting the urge to put his side of the story down in some form or other.

A chance meeting at the Crystal Palace with James Jones the writer of *From Here to Eternity*, and Lorney Handy, the woman who had inspired Jones at her writing school in Illinois, gave him the encouragement to go ahead.

Jay organised himself. Days for the Galleries, evenings till 9 p.m. at the typewriter and then after 9 p.m. at the Palace trying to keep his writing secret. Sort of.

He had a title. *The Nervous Set*. An opening line. 'You can't stay married if you want to make it in New York.' And injection-fuelled recollections that needed careful handling.

But meanwhile in the life he was living, Jay was having a bout of unusual guilt pangs which had everything to do with Fran. He was beginning to recognise that despite his open challenges to the conventions of sex, marriage and infidelity he had pushed Fran into a conventional life of accepting this as a man's prerogative and that a woman to play the same game would make her a home breaker.

It seemed right on the many nights when cocktail hour bewitched the senses and the tongue but as he sat writing it came across as increasingly destructive.

And Fran was hardly unaware of what was going on. In her capacity of floor manager at the Palace she was meeting the entertainers who came to play on the little stage, one of whom was a little known piano player called Tommy Wolf. He had a way with the tunes of the day and was a clever improviser on them. Together one day they came up with a hip line that would become her signature and their best known collaboration. 'Spring can really hang you up the most.' It became a wistful and plaintive hymn to the life she was leading and it couldn't have failed to give Jay a jolt. And reminder:

> All alone, the party's over
> Old Man Winter was a gracious host
> But when you keep praying for snow to hide the clover
> Spring can really hang you up the most

Fran got pregnant. Or maybe I could say that Jay woke up.

For a while things went well and a peaceful family life ensued. That is, as far as an inveterate bar hound like Jay could make it happen. Fran could still legitimately complain:

'Bar talk, bar talk. That's all you and your friends ever talk about.' Well, what else do you expect a dog to do?

But that would prove to be a brief respite from real life as Fran would miscarriage, for the second time, and plunge her into a deep depression. It didn't leave Jay in a much better state and this would be reflected in the final scenes of *The Nervous Set*, where the meaty pleasure principal and the bony cynicism suddenly turned black and bloody.

Meantime....

The Crystal Palace was booming.

O'Neil had become the talk of the town with his manicured fingernails and masterful control of the customers that flocked to the hippest bar in the city. While everyone who came in had to wear a tie it didn't mean that the style was straight. Romance flourished and lust was approved of, with every available darkened corner and cranny used to encourage the fingers to do the walking. If you wanted to take a piss in the toilet it was a challenge to your bladder.

Some beautiful things about St Louis: TOP outside the Crystal Palace; MIDDLE inside the Crystal Palace; BOTTOM Mrs William Rhinelander Stewart – the lady wants to be amused.

There were better uses for that space. The cloakroom was not only for coats and the space behind the ice cube maker had its charms.

The combination of gold trim, crystal reflections where ever you looked, 50 varieties of splendid whiskey, the evocative piano and the black painted brick sent people into spasms of sensual riot which Jay actively encouraged and explored and O'Neil liberally fuelled for his open ended observations on the drinking man's culture.

This was a bar for the hedonists and not the faint hearted.

Talking of faint hearted. That unfortunately was the response Jay got when he sent *The Nervous Set* manuscript to New York. Rinehart, the publisher had been recommended to Jay by his old friend Brossard. What he didn't know was that Stanley Rinehart had recently rejected Norman Mailer's *The Deer Park* because it was 'a dirty book'. While the editor, who tried to get the project going, thought: 'Your book is the kind that makes my bosses very uncomfortable; it reminds them of the truth about themselves and the world they live in,' the editor in chief would sentence it as: 'trash and I don't want to hear any more of it'

The very publishing establishment that had watched in disbelief as *Neurotica* not only found a niche but also opened up a can of new visions, was now pleased to let the editor and publisher of that magazine know that his insiders view of the flotsam and jetsam of intellectual life in New York was not going to be published in their houses under any circumstances.

Jay was absolutely rejected. No surprise there. Shame really, but it was still only 1954.

It was a hot summer in St Louis and Jay now had a new project to fool around with. It was called the Advanced School of Cultural Analysis. It was announced thus: 'Beat the heat with ASCA, the University of the Imagination. Free martinis served before, during and after each lecture.'

These were going to be a series of seminars on the more important aspects of modern American culture to be held in a little, air conditioned cinema down the road from the Crystal Palace.

Today I lick my lips at the thought of an invitation like that.

Then it also proved irresistible. An assortment of Jay's buddies, lecturers drawn from the ranks of the C. P. cocktail hour and 'professors of cultural relevancy' tempted from out of town, came to sample the quirkily titled seminars and free drinks.

'Squaresville USA: A New Look at Main Street,' 'Modern Music and Nerve Endings,' 'Abortive Attempts at Middleclass Rebellion,' 'How Deep is My Funk' and the final lecture by Jay…'American Culture is Here to Stay: How to Live With It.'

The series caught the attention of the director of the local educational TV, who bravely offered Jay a chance to bring the format to his television audience. Everyone was beginning to see the potential for cultural confluence. Mark the name of the show: *Off Beat: An Excursion Down Cultural Bypaths.*

The show opened with the camera moving up Jay's stove pipe legs, past his daring black hopsacking suit to a head shot of the man saying: 'Talk is cheap, so here I am.' A line that still hasn't been improved on (after 50 years) to get your audience to think why they are watching you in the first place. By the end of the first show Jay and his guests had woken up St Louis. The switchboard jammed with cries of horror at the variously, communist, faggot, racist, un-American, disgusting, unchristian, family hating sum bitches. In sum, a success.

As summer gave way to autumn Jay was preparing for another major production. The man just couldn't keep his fingers in one pie. But this time he was part of a double act. He finally was going to become a father. Fran had gone through her pregnancy without a hitch. And Jay had added to the sense that maybe he was going to finally grow up by buying a house for his little family.

The child was a boy and the boy was called Cosmo. I know… poor kid.

Maybe Jay consulted his Jewish oracle and discovered something the rest of the world couldn't figure out. My guess is that he bit off half a word he liked and likened himself to – cosmopolitan – and thought it would be a gift for a child that would become in time as the definition has it – 'free from national limitations or prejudices'. Cosmo.

'Everything flows and nothing stays...
you can't step twice into the same river'
(Heraclitus)

Jay was keeping occupied. He had converted flats above the Landesman. Galleries into a number of studios that were meant to attract
the young entrepreneurs and sophisticated people with a penchant
for the unorthodox into the area. The turn of the century style that
the neighbourhood had been famous for, was gradually revitalised
as new bars and restaurants moved into Bed Bug Row. There was
room, for everyone no matter how outlandish their ideas. It was that
wonderful time called 'creation of a cool place' before it becomes
'speculation for profit.' Anything goes. The area got a new name,
Gaslight Square, and St Louis was beginning to show signs of developing a seriously interesting night life.

But that meant more serious competition for the Crystal Palace
and for the services of their celebrity barman Jack O'Neil. Because
that is what he had become. He now had a hard core fan base that
wanted him not only at cocktail hour but also took him out to lunch
and even flew him to New York for private, functions. He had been
one of the more provocative acts on Jay's television show with his
idea of making a mock cookery program illustrating the stratifica-
tion of American society by making salads with the ingredients that
illustrated his pungent opinions.

It was time to get away from bartenders, to shows. O'Neil
finally defected to one of the new bars opening up but by then Jay
had come back from a trip to Chicago with what he was looking
for: The Compass Players, a group of improvisational actors (a rare
beast in those days of music hail cabaret acts), under the direc-
tion of Theodore J. Flicker, who had the idea of playing in night
clubs all over America. The Crystal Palace would be their testing
ground.

Lovers of the new comedy scene today would recognise this approach to drama and humour, but it was a shock to the system in 1955. No one in the audience would ever have forgotten its impact.

The stage was dark. Two of the players were planted in the audience. They began to argue until the rest of the audience were shouting at them to shut up. As the couple made their way to the stage, Flicker, a small volatile man with a Mephistopheles beard, dressed in a black leotard, hopped on to the stage and shouted 'Freeze!' The lights went up on the performers. 'What happens next?' he asked the audience. 'C'mon, you tell us.'

Social satire had arrived and something new was happening in entertainment in America. But the material really hotted up when Mike Nichols (eventually to become an Oscar winning film director) and Elaine May (eventually to become a famous scriptwriter as well a film director) came down as a team from Chicago. The pair of them were lethal. They were already seasoned performers and masters of improvisation and their material carried the seeds of the aggressive and sharp social humour that would characterise the next decade, the 1960s.

A production of *Waiting for Godot*, one of the first anywhere in the world outside New York, would be well received by an audience that was getting to expect unusual treats from Jay and his cohorts as they kept on challenging the conventions where ever they found them. So the Crystal Palace had just about everything you would want from a bar. Bartenders (now sans O'Neil) who worked the drinks with efficiency and interest. Music to get you in the mood. A scent of sensuality permanently in the air. In an aesthetically seductive environment. That encouraged sex. That encouraged an open mind. Kept open by provocative shows. And led with bravado by Jay.

But actually there was something missing. Size. It ain't everything as everybody loves pointing out but in this case there was a point to it.

Their phenomenal success started them thinking in terms of bigger productions with their own theatre company. They needed to

find a place where they could seat three hundred. Then they would
do original and experimental theatre for 32 weeks and the rest of
the time Jay would produce cabaret, revues and bring in some star
attractions..

It was going to be financially risky but everyone was in perfect
agreement that the time was right and the need was there for this to
work. New York would deny it years later but the biggest balls in the
land were at this time (1958) to be found in St Louis.

Jay Landesman now had a new calling card. The Producer.

A series of wild nights heralded the closing of the old Palace, with
E. T. Trova painting extraordinary pictures while the band played,
and then auctioning off the results to the punters. A site for the new
Crystal Palace Cabaret Theatre was finally found, in the heart of
Gaslight Square.

The lights went out at the Bar.

And on at the new Crystal Palace Theatre Bar.

What emerged was a cross between a church and a movie palace... without the reverence. The walls and ceilings were painted fire
engine red, casting, as was intended, an unearthly glow, reinforced
by a 50 foot mural of church stained glass lit from behind and complete with 'in memoriam' notices. Purgatorial messages perhaps but
the necessary touch of frivolity came from especially designed, huge
crystal and brass chandeliers.

'If they don't like the show they can always look at the chandeliers,' said brother Fred. Now all they needed were plays that could
compete with the decor.

That proved to be a problem. One avant-garde play by Brossard,
one adaptation by Peter Stone of a Dostoevsky novel and one *End-
game* by Beckett later they realised they would be facing financial
ruin if they didn't find the right pulse of the crowd. Sure they loved
the novelty of drinking while watching a play but maybe the fare was
all a bit too heavy for them. After all this was St Louis and not Paris.

Flicker had an idea. 'I know what we'll do gang. Let's put on a
musical.'

But what would be a suitable musical to put on at a place like the Crystal Palace? Home to an *Oklahoma* it wasn't. What was proposed was to use the Landesman–Wolf songbook as the basis of a show.

Do you remember Fran and Tommy Wolf putting together 'Spring really hangs you up the most' back in the early days of the Crystal Palace Bar? Well they had come a long way since those days. Recordings of 'Spring' had been done by Ella Fitzgerald, Sarah Vaughn, Jackie Cain and others and they were now established as a serious song writing team. But was there a book to base the show on? Ah, as it so happened there was. *The Nervous Set.* Jay's manuscript. The Zeitgeist was there. Since Jay had tried to have it published, the whole scene he had observantly written about had become the latest sensation with the publication of Kerouac's *On the Road* as well as Ginsberg, Holmes and Brossard all having come through as celebrities from those Beat Times.

But Jay wasn't too sure this had the right legs on it. Though it certainly captured the atmosphere of those early Beatnik days in the Village, the above mentioned were only peripheral to the story of Fran and him trying to survive those *Neurotica* days with just Legman as the other main character.

Flicker asked to read it. Jay with some trepidation gave it to him. 24 hours later Flicker was back at his house. 'This is it my boy. It's going to make us all rich and famous.' Jay would've kissed him but mindful of his reputation bought him a cup of coffee instead and put out his hand for the golden handshake.

Flicker, Fran and Jay collaborated on it together. The songs were easy to find as Fran's lyrics were all about her life with Jay and many of them were of *The Nervous Set* period. The fact that there private life was going up for public scrutiny on stage didn't seem to have a particularly fearful element for them. But of course, only if it was a success. I don't suppose you put up your dirty washing on a line unless it is peculiarly interesting...

The Nervous Set opened on March 4, 1959. It was an instant success. That included Fran's parents strangely enough, Cutie, Jay's mother, who never the less complained that the cast was badly dressed but most importantly, *Variety's* man in St Louis who gave it a review that attracted New York producers immediately:

'*The Nervous Set*, a locally written musical comedy, has premiered at the Crystal Palace saloon theatre to ecstatic packed house enthusiasm... *The Nervous Set* deals with the beat generation, sometimes tenderly, sometimes spicily, sometimes hilariously, but always entertainingly... Mrs Landesman's lyrics and Tommy Wolf's music are polished to a fine sheen, either on the tender Spring Can Really Hang You Up The Most, or the ribald chant, How Do You Like Your Love?... The musical numbers punctuate a tragicomic scene that shifts back and forth from square Connecticut to beat Greenwich Village to Manhattan's stony Sutton Place... The appealing hero and heroine are storm tossed between the wacky world of the editor's milieu and the sane domesticity the girl craves... although there are some shining moments of pathos, hilarity is always just round the corner...'

Well doesn't that sound just like the times I have shown you in Jay's World?

It looked like clear sailing all the way to the Bank and Beyond... Broadway perhaps?

But where there is a Jay there is a way to make you want to call off all bets on the certainty factor. Jay had in fact signed a contract early on with Flicker that stipulated that he would direct the show if it ever got to Broadway, something Jay was comfortable with seeing how the man had whipped the show into such fine shape. The problem was the Broadway producers who were interested, Alexander Cohen and Saint-Subber, insisted that Flicker should not be part of the package (shades of the *Neurotica* deal) even though they were talking in terms of an original cast album. On the other hand there was a charming agent, called Robert Lantz, who was associated with big Hollywood films who was happy to have Flicker on board just so long as there were a few cast changes and a different ending. 'Broadway is not ready for a musical ending with a suicide,' he told them wisely. The icing on the cake was David Merrick who told Jay not to do anything till he had the chance to come down and see the show. The scene was set for Jay to use all the lessons he had learned, to fine tune his instincts on the timing for this deal to work. But he also had a wife with a rather different set of priorities, who was ready to go to New York immediately and strike while the iron was hot, encouraged by Lantz. He had been calling from New York with siren talk of immediate recording deals with Columbia Records, if they closed down the show at the Crystal Palace and brought it over to New York and, of course, accepted the necessary changes in the story. Jay had the feeling that she would walk over his dead body if he refused.

'Listen Jay, if you don't give me this opportunity, I'll never forgive you. What do you know about show business? They're the professionals. Leave it to them.'

Jay on the other hand was sure that if they tried to tweak the show around to suit a Broadway formula it would fall apart. David Merrick had been put on hold which was no way to treat the great man. Plus, the show was making a very sizeable sum of money for the Crystal Palace and demand was increasing all the time. On asking Martha Gelhorn's mother, a grand dowager on the St Louis society scene since the turn of the century, why she was coming to see the show for the second time, she said simply: 'It is the story of my life'. And that was its secret ingredient. Everyone who saw it either imagined a life like that with fascination, aspired to a glittering madness like *The Nervous Set* or in fact had an under-the-sheets version of it going on.

Fred in the end put Jay out of his misery.

'Listen Jay. If you hold it up from going to Broadway, you'll have a crazy woman on your hands.' He paused like the good brother he was. 'For life'.

All the martinis in the world were not prepared to give him a better diagnosis. The rest of his world was not supporting him either. It was now or never. Sometimes true indeed...

Well, they were the experts. He was just an antique salesman. He signed the contacts with Lantz.

NEW YORK

"Raffishly comic!" - Atkinson ☺ "Sharp and satirical!" - Watts ☺ "Filled with creepy creeps, nasty-tongued, dirty-minded and dirty-clothed. They are depressed and depressing!" - Coleman ☺ "The freshest satire on current manners New York has seen all season!" - Atkinson ☺ "This score just plain doesn't give a damn about verses and choruses and tunes and it is therefore uncommonly interesting!" - Chapman ☺ "Cool beatnik bid often a gasser!" - Mc Clain ☺ "The beatnik mind is now within inches of the fifth-rate work of the early 'twenties!" - Kerr ☺

What New York critics said about *The Nervous Set.*

'One finger in the throat and one in the rectum makes a good diagnostician' (W. Osler)

The musical was scheduled to open at the Henry Miller Theatre in New York on May 11, 1959. Another springtime date in Jay's calendar.

The fun part was having a specially designed suit for the occasion which involved twenty fittings and a virtual nervous breakdown by the master tailor before completing a complicated cut to his trousers which included a 'Trevor Howard pleated front' and a 'George Raft back' with a serious novelty in buttoned flies. The suit was dark blue, soft wool pinstripe with padded shoulders and a 1920s orange Parker pen in the breast pocket. A suit ahead of its time. Tailoring for a man to celebrate the absurd.

The producer, Lantz, wanted to make more than a few changes. Even the title was in jeopardy. Lantz was a Hungarian immigrant who felt that his mission was to explain America to the Americans. Not the first European to want to do that and not the last either. Jay, as a second generation American and fully paid up member of *The Nervous Set* felt he was closer to the answer So key songs and episodes and cast members were fought over.

When Fran and Jay had driven to New York in his convertible Packard with the thoughts of a possible hit on Broadway, Jay had reflected with a wry grin on the departure 7 years earlier in his old touring car with the sun setting on his New York ambitions But a lot of water had passed under that bridge as well and while he was now the father of two boys (oh yes, another kid called Miles had been born the previous year; he went easy on that name), his relationship with Fran was an uneasy one. Like the sign advertising the show at the Henry Miller said: book by Jay Landesman but the lyrics were by Fran Landesman.

He was writing the story on open marriage arrangements but Fran was writing the poetry that spelt out the effect this was having on their emotional landscape.

By the time of the three preview nights, the show had three different endings with a cast designed to highlight and mock the excesses of *The Nervous Set* rather than to show them to be a vibrant though offbeat slice of big city Americana.

Jay was no longer consulted, as director and producer searched for the formula that would make the musical a Broadway success He let them get on with it and tried not to vomit every night before going to bed. Even dreamy Fran was suspecting that this highjack was going to turn into a revisionist hell.

The big night arrived. For the first time in years Jay saw Kerouac again. Royally drunk and bellicose he wanted to check if Jay had done a number on him. But it was good to see a son of the beatnik time there beside him to counterpoint the well-dressed friends who had poured out of St Louis to see their favourite son conquer Broadway.

First night audiences are not the people you take judgements from as they are mainly friends and backers, but when the show had ended Jay got the drift of the mood that confirmed his depressed judgement that the 'Broadway Professionals' had massacred his story. When Cutie cut to the chase in the restaurant after the show saying: 'It was better in St Louis' he knew that he had been shafted.

As is traditional they waited around for the first newspaper reviews. The first paper to arrive was the *New York Times* with Brook Atkinson's review, who was thought to make or break shows. His was a fulsomely complimentary review only complaining about the false ending. There were cheers all round. For the next 10 minutes New York was an exciting and wonderful place to be in for Jay who revived his dream of moving to the city with Fran, writing more shows, living in a penthouse and drinking with the top culturati dogs.

And then the rottweilers arrived. Each review was worse than the one before. 'This theatre-goer found himself out in left field not digging a lick of it.' '*The Nervous Set* makes me wonder if I am really an old poop.' 'One of those rumpuses that will either irritate you or fascinate you. It irritated us enormously.' 'The cast should have their mouths washed out with soap for singing Mrs Landesman's lyrics.' And so on and so forth.

Jay was stunned to find that their spoof, tongue in cheek, beatnik musical was being taken so seriously. But hey when you want to take on the prevailing tides you got to have a wise tiller-man who knows how the winds work. But they didn't have one. Only the hot air of the show's publicist remained to keep them from heading straight onto the rocks.

The people who might have been drawn out of curiosity to the show, if there had been enough interested reviews stayed away in their droves. It just wasn't fashionable to 'do beatnik' any more. The idea of someone bothering to satirise them was inconceivable to a world that had moved on back to crew cuts, cheer leaders and gin and tonics.

It's fair to say that Jay's sails were well and truly shredded. Fran was still trying to put the cast through their recording paces but our man had nowhere to go.

Two very subdued Broadway rejects arrived back in St Louis.

Throughout that summer the show struggled to survive but even though some social commentators gave it good marks for perception and wit, it was dying a lonely death. The cast album got good reviews but again there were no phone calls from New York asking for their services.

Jay had put one finger to his throat and found the evidence unpalatable. Now he was going to try the other finger (for those who don't follow my drift just check the headlining quotation at the beginning of this piece).

He figured he had found a new musical Fran and him could work on together. It would be based on Nelson Algren's novel *A Walk On The Wild Side*. It had Jay's favourite theme: the Horatio Alger myth, but in reverse. The hero comes to the big city and goes down the ladder of success. Jay felt it bore a more than passing resemblance to his attempts to conquer New York and so felt drawn to it.

Nelson Algren was equally drawn to Fran's lyrics so after setting up a meeting they all fell on the project with a shared passion. The score was again by Tommy Wolf and it was enthusiastically previewed to Algren and his friends.

But unfortunately Jay's script was given the thumbs down by Algren who it seemed wanted something more akin to 'real life'. Jay doesn't do 'real life' very well. It isn't that he doesn't know about it, it's more that he isn't a part of it. Let us not forget our man here.

So Algren rewrote the book, making the hero out of a minor character without any legs and populated the show with pimps, whores, criminals, beggars, drunkards and all, who sang and danced their way through one of the more grotesque and depressing evenings the Crystal Palace had ever seen. But with a big name like Nelson Algren at the helm, Jay was able to call David Merrick to come to see it and, much to his surprise, he said he would. It was a night of one of the worst blizzards ever seen, but the great St Louis-born producer duly arrived. Jay and company had managed, it seemed, to have stored up some credit from their abortive Broadway venture, and the cast came out with all guns blazing which left everyone in no doubt that there was a show here. But for whom?

Merrick insisted on leaving that night, even though it would be by bus. He confided to Jay that he absolutely detested the city and nothing would induce him to stay. But before he left, while complimenting the cast and all who had worked on the production, he made his feelings clear that while he thought it was a good show, 'It's not my kind of musical'.

The next weeks proved in fact that it really wasn't anybody's kind of musical.

It was time for Jay to take his finger out, take the sting out of failure and get back to some uncomplicated fun.

'His imagination resembled the wings of an ostrich. It enabled him to run though not to soar' *(Lord Macauley)*

After taking a trip through Europe to get the St Louis Blues out of their system Jay and Fran returned to the city to prepare themselves for what the new decade would bring. This was now 1960. While enjoying Paris and being delighted by La Dolce Vita of Rome, it was London that had made Jay's heart sing. He felt at home with the first stirrings of the Angry Young Men who were using the American Beats as the template for the challenges they had in mind for British society. It definitely smelt to Jay's refined nose for anticipating social changes, that there would be some serious mischief making to be found in London Town in the not too distant future.

Nevertheless he was now back in St Louis wondering how he was going to help his kids answer the question, 'and what does your father do for a living?'. When a man reaches the age of forty there usually is an answer. But Jay had moved from his early days of being an antique dealer to publisher, editor, novelist, playwright, TV personality, entrepreneur, theatrical producer and not forgetting, urban renewal expert.

Gaslight Square was growing at an unbelievable rate. Jay formed a loose organisation to keep the professionals out. No strippers, no hustlers, no clip joints and no sleazy premises were allowed. He petitioned the city to change the name of the area officially to Gaslight Square and talked the local gas company into restoring the original gas lights.

Urban planners from other cities in America came to see and ask for advice on how to build up similar areas in their cities. In fact if Jay had been any more professional he could probably have made a fortune in the advisory business. But he could only consult in his own fashion which included too much, unasked for, honesty in his appraisals. It was all too much of a gas for the gaslight square entrepreneur.

About this time Jay and Fran finally put their cards on the table and played out a full hand of truth or consequences about their extra-marital affairs. They were both unpleasantly surprised by the extent of their mutual unfaithfulness but by the same token, since they were both sexual criminals, there was no punishment to fit the crime.

In fact, it was a relief to Jay, in particular, to find that he had lost his exclusive right to the double-standard clause in the marriage contract.

Jay's career as an adulterer, unfortunately, was proving more successful than his career as a theatrical producer. The crowds coming to the Gaslight Square had changed considerably. They didn't want to be educated with original plays, like Mailer's *The Deer Park*, Ionesco's *The Chairs*, Beckett's *Krapp's Last Tape*; they preferred the entertainment from the cabaret season.

Jay produced a steady stream of highly satirical revues that were always topical. *Love, Money and Fame* proved to be just as successful as *The Nervous Set*. *Hostilities in 1961* captured the mood of the times and *New Directions* pointed, as always with Jay, to a vision of an unlikely future that could actually be true.

Of course there had to be some prime players to make this scene happen and perhaps the most emblematic of these characters would be Lenny Bruce. Bruce was just getting into his 'take no prisoners' phase and it suited the Crystal Palace like a well-fitting condom The dirtier he got the more the audience lapped it up. Even Jay got into the act, by taking longer every time he came to introduce Bruce, so that the intro became a warm up act all on its own. That didn't particularly go down well with the man renowned for biting the hand that fed him… still, Jay survived, but in the process becoming addicted to the microphone and experiencing the novelty of having the freedom to say anything he wanted.

Heady times for a man enamoured with the workings of his own tongue under normal circumstances...

The drama critic of the *St Louis Post Dispatch* was moved to say: 'It was apparent that the loud laughter Landesman received went to his head. I am afraid that last night an incurable ham was born and in gaining a comedian, we have lost a producer.'

When the Palace bought out the last remaining old time neighbourhood bar next door, they put in a little stage to do late night cabaret and recreate the relaxed atmosphere of the old Crystal Palace, as well as to catch the overflow from the crowds waiting for the big room act to begin.

This is where Jay started testing his theory that there was as much an art to making rejection work for you as there was fun in failure. His material consisted of stories of the heroic failures in his life starting with his childhood. It wasn't the standard approach to humour in those days so it wasn't surprising that after awhile the waitresses went to brother Fred with a petition: 'Get him off the stage or we quit. He's emptying the room and we're not getting any tips.'

Phyllis Diller, who was one of the few comediennes around, and specialised in cringe making self deprecating humour, was even moved to tell Jay: 'I don't think the American people are ready for you yet.'

But rejection was never going to make Jay crack up... even though it didn't seem to make his audience crack up either. Embarrassment was just not built into the man's nature.

The truth was that by now Jay was a regular fixture in the social pages, gossip columns and the must-be-seen in parties. The night club world was his social passport which he used liberally. Making trips to New York to look for talent, he would visit other clubs and make himself comfortable with their clientele, lingering at tables of performers or their agents just long enough to let them know who he was. This was the fine art of 'working a room' which was tailor made for a man who could stroke a pussy at the same time that he looked a king in the eye.

One of the agents, Irwin Arthur, known as the 'Prince of Darkness', because of his sometime shady dealings cornered Jay one day with a proposition that seemed easy to turn down:

'Got a winner for you. She's just your style, crazy and cheap and I'll give you options when she's a star. Get her now while she's available. Her name is Barbara Streisand.'

Well Jay wasn't too enthused when he heard that this 18 year old had never worked in a night club, had done one Jack Parr show with a good response (her agent would say that wouldn't he?), a funny face and a nose that you had to see to believe. Her saving grace appeared to be a great voice and the fact that she knew Fran's songs. He decided that she would be part of a revue format with the Smothers Brothers, who at the time were yet to break into television, but were the big names and Jay with his intro patter that had become a tiny thing of beauty (at least to its presenter), calling it *Caught in the Act.*

You could say that Jay rescued Barbara Streisand from herself as she had the habit of going into a Jewish mama routine between songs that detracted from her singing. Jay gave her the advice to stick to the songs and let him do the funny stuff...

So one of them went on to become world famous. And the other...? Wait and see.

Jay continued producing the satirical revues that anatomised the taboos still prevalent in marriage, the family, careers, sex politics and success. Among the acts he got for a show called *Stars of Tomorrow* was an insecure and permanently nervous young man from New York, called Woody Allen. Already well known as a writer, he was at the Palace to break in his stand up comic material. He was the funniest performer Jay had ever seen but after every show, Allen would dash to the public phone by the toilets to call his psychiatrist in New York and go through his catalogue of insecurities. It was as funny to listen to him there as it was to catch his act on stage. The laughs from the toilet queues encouraged him somewhat, but he would have preferred to be back on the couch instead of on the phone. 'For one thing, it's a lot cheaper than these long distance phone calls.'

Jay and Woody weren't cut from the same Jewish cloth but they both had a take on failure inspired by their mothers. The difference was that while Woody was a wonderfully funny performer but a sad sack in life, Jay was wonderfully expressive in life but unable to find the material for his comic aspirations. Hey, you win some or you're handsome.

The Crystal Palace was still growing, keeping up with the rapidly changing times and the new developments in the Gaslight Square. They opened a summer outdoor garden of delights with stained glass hanging from the trees and hanging lanterns over a barbecue pit, as well as building a dance floor and putting in a rock band to entice the younger people who were flocking to the area.

There were now over twenty clubs and bars offering everything and anything that would attract the crowds. The days of having the Square to themselves were over. Music began to blare from loud speakers up and down the streets.

Jay was still involved, trying to keep the identity of Gaslight Square alive with the influx of the new professionals, straightening out problems that success was bringing to the community. He self-lessly became a trouble shooter and advisor to all those trying to get a handle on the Square. It was as if the rest of St Louis didn't really count... which to many people was exactly the truth of the matter. Gaslight Square was the heart of the city, the Crystal Palace was its most precious jewel and Jay was the ringmaster.

Time magazine saw the American success story there. Under the headline 'No Squares On The Square' their team of reporters summed up what had happened:

> In the gazetteer of U.S. nightlife, St Louis has never been placed high... most of St Louis spends its evenings the way most of the rest of the U.S. does: watching television or drinking beer in somebody else's living room.

But now all that has changed. St Louis finally has a place to go at night and the place is Gaslight Square...

A three-block oasis of nostalgic frivolity where some fifty gaudily atmospheric taverns, cabarets, restaurants and antique shops are packed together in fine, fin-de-siècle jumble, it combines the gaiety of Copenhagen's Tivoli Gardens and the innocent naughtiness of Gay Nineties beer halls., with property values tripling over the last four years... Jay Landesman has been voted unofficial mayor of the quarter. Says Landesman grandly: 'It means nothing. I'd rather be king...'

The kiss of death moves in mysterious ways. You wouldn't have thought that a top review at a capital moment was in effect the last peak in the experience.

Jay was enjoying the hospitality of the great and the good and also all the bastards who now were prepared to overlook his Jewish ancestry. There was nothing much wrong with his social life.

But in an attempt to keep up with the young trend setters he found that he had opened up a can of worms. Dumbing down is what we would call it today.

Always looking to keep the edge on the competition but also to keep the punters keen with new thrills, Jay opened the first 'Twist Room in the West' as that dance craze began to sweep through the young things who were now beyond mere bop and rock. He may have been 45 now but that didn't stop Jay from being the king of the floor, as he and the sexiest waitress at the Palace, demonstrated the moves in an exhibition area in the Annex. Not only were people trying it out but passers-by stopped to gawk at this weird concoction lead by the 'Grand Master Twister' himself.

The policy of lightening the fare at the Palace was extended to the theatre as the audiences became less interested in discriminating and challenging fare, and showed their preferences for melodramas and light entertainment where critics could use terms like 'king sized laughs' and 'it was a great old time meller dramer with villains to be hissed and slinky sirens to be admired.'

It made the bank manager happy but it didn't put a smile on Jay's face. Serious theatre was going the way of the Dodo.

Old friends returned to the cabaret, but the ones whose material depended on manic topicality like Lenny Bruce, were having a harder time of it, The Smothers Brothers, on the other hand, were becoming seriously famous with their brand of quirky humour and gentle musical satire. Barbara Streisand tried but failed to get a return booking at the Palace. Jay's nose told him that she wasn't ready yet for his establishment.

Visits to New York were no longer to look for talent but more to have a chance to reminisce about the 'good old days 'with those who were still alive and those who weren't lost to the 'name game'.

Fran had composed a particularly sharp observation about these gatherings called 'The Ballad Of The Sad Young Men':

All the sad young men
Sitting in the bars
Knowing neon lights
Missing all the stars...
Autumn turns the leaves to gold
Slowly dies the heart
Sad young men are growing old
That's the cruelest part...

Jay Landesman was not a sad young man. He was a youthful and fun-loving 45 year old with a penchant for the lovely young ladies that the entertainment business attracted by the bus load. But he was also a married man with two kids. And his wife was no stay-at-home southern belle but an equally raunchy though melancholic and gifted lyricist. The fact that they had a family psychiatrist on retainer didn't mean that all that was broken was getting mended.

He still saw himself as a rebel for whom nothing was sacred and everyone was fair game. That is not an uncommon assumption by those who have succeeded in inventing a persona for themselves where there is no sense of responsibility to anything or anyone else unless it comes wrapped in applause or gives cause to party.

The curious thing though was that Jay never thought for a moment that Fran was anything other than a permanent fixture in his life. In fact neither one ever thought of leaving the other. They were just going to have to work this out together. Which is what they did. It got messy at times and there was blood letting, but in the end after running through a series of psychiatrists and marriage councillors and their assistants, they found blue sky.

It was a form of 'open marriage', a concept yet to be understood by the majority, while the minority would have to wait for Masters and Johnson to come along a couple of years later, before recognising what their sexual experiments could lead to.

Fran and Jay came to realise that they were committed practitioners of the 'let's have our cake and eat it too' school and they gave each other licence to do just that. They were embracing a hedonism that would become the lynchpin of all that would characterise the late sixties and seventies. Jay's Way.

Curtain Call at the Crystal Palace

It didn't take Jay booking Gypsy Rose Lee for a two week engagement, to discover that his time in the sun was about over. After all his campaigning to keep strippers from the Square it seemed like the height of hypocrisy, even though the lady hadn't shed so much as a glove in the previous twenty years. It was just time to 'get' the previously untouchable Palace.

I suppose there is only so long you can navigate against the prevailing ethos of a city before you start getting a backlash. Especially if you are a few years short of the times when you would be in your natural element. The Gaslight Square was really a creature of the late sixties for a big city and of the eighties for a provincial city like St Louis.

After the first mugging in the vicinity of the Square was followed by a murder not far away, people woke up to the fact that the neighbourhood that surrounded it was not salubrious and in fact was still decaying and developing the first signs of racial tension. The Palace's audience had grown older and in some cases grown up with the Square, but were now jaded by its offerings and more concerned for their personal safety and youth culture was heading in directions the Palace couldn't take them. Street action was where it was at and not acts to be found in the cabaret or theatre. So the oasis of unconventional razzmatazz and orgasmic alternatives found that it was coarsening the product to get at those unconvinced palates.

By the time Jay found himself booking a belly-dancing troupe as his top drawing act... and thinking they were a great novelty... he knew that there weren't going to be too many more martinis at the Crystal Palace for him.

The zeitgeist has only a limited life span. The summer of '64 would prove to be the end of the show at the Crystal Palace for Jay. After 12 years of producing shows, he was creatively exhausted. But without the Palace he didn't see any future for himself in St Louis. It would have been as if he had trapped himself in the real world and that was no place for a man like him to retire in.

New York was a possibility. Certainly it would give Fran, who by now was a recognised song-writing talent, a chance to promote her career in Manhattan... but what would the husband do? There wasn't a big call on Jay's talents for some reason.

Exotic options always came up with the same conundrum. Would his sanity prevail if he became a country gentleman with no visible means of support? It was not a scenario Jay, consummate city boy, could really take on board. On top of which Fran had categorically warned him that: 'I don't want to go any place where they don't speak English'.

England seemed the perfect answer. And London the perfect place. It was taking off, it had new and experimental theatres, and best of all it had people who had yet to experience the Fran and Jay show. Let's be fair... who had yet to meet Jay Landesman.

When the St Louis newspapers heard they were going to London, they wrote it up as a news feature: 'Landesmans To London For Talent Tune Up'. But the real story came out in an article by the arts editor:

> Now Jay and Fran Landesman are leaving town and their going marks the end of an Era – the Era of The Crystal Palace and High Style. They are leaving with no boo-hoos, no bitterness, but with a little sadness and a touch of puzzlement. They are not leaving for a better offer. They are leaving to get away from us and take a look around another town... What are they worth to us? What did they cost that we were not willing to pay? All of us, those who love them and those who are saying good riddance, have been enriched by them. We become a little more drab as we wave goodbye.

The Fun was Done in St Louis.
'Leave them while you are looking good.'

'And Now For Something Completely Different.' (Graham Chapman)

Americans in the early sixties travelled with trepidation or with wide eyed innocence to England and to its enchanted capital city. Unless you were a cocky New Yorker or a Hollywood film star the reception you received could make you feel like a hick or a virgin at a whore's ball. The class system which kept most people in their appointed place ran totally counter to the American system which was to give pride of place to the man with the biggest wallet.

What sort of American was Jay Landesman, late of St Louis and uncrowned king of a time and place that had about as much relevance to 1964 London as a street map of Gaslight Square?

He had no Hollywood pedigree. He was not a New York player. He didn't carry a big wallet.

He was a middle aged Beatnik and Hipster in a time when the accent on rebellious youth was beginning to rear its alien head.

He was loud and garrulous in a land where people still kept their emotions buttoned up. He was a man who had always had a court to play up to but who was now in a land where people took a lifetime assessing whether you were friend material.

Hey, was Jay going to be able to cut the mustard?

The original plan was to stay a year and see whether the social climate suited his health. Fran and the kids were going to take their medicine in their own ways… as always.

We know the man was enterprising so if the balloon went up it would be with the panache of a *Titanic* passenger getting the waiter to fill his glass as the ship sank under the waves.

An ad in *The Times* got the ball rolling. 'American author desperately needs flat with character to rent…' What he found at the Angel in Islington was a maisonette in a Georgian terrace filled with enough antiques to make the family feel at home. A statue of a reclining lion guarded the entrance, which was just as well as the Angel in those days was a place of dubious reputation still bearing the scars of the blitz. But then the early days in Gaslight Square had hardly been in a salubrious place either. The difference was that that had been Jay's back yard while this was something he had only ever seen before on a black and white postcard. The sort you receive from a friend with a strange sense of humour.

Along with that novelty were of course the other eye openers, like the lack of showers in bathrooms with odd taps and toilets that gargled like hungry beasts when you flushed them coal burning stoves and open fireplaces that needed 24 hour attention to keep the damp from eating through your bones; food that they were accustomed to was just not available and the food they did find they had no name for; the electric appliances taken for granted in the States seemed not to have been invented yet in England.

But on the other hand Jay found politeness in the streets and in his dealing with people that quite startled him. How many 'thank yous' can you use in a simple transaction was a question that fascinated him. And of course to Jay's eye, the denizens of the area were all the sorts of characters that films of Dickensian England had prepared him to enjoy and want to interact with. Street theatre at its most enchanting. The only entry he had into the arty society of London was Peter Cook's telephone number, given to him by the poet Adrian Mitchell, who he had met in New York. Cook had just closed down his club, The Establishment, which had been doing the job in London that the Crystal Palace had done in St Louis, so there was a symbiotic relationship between them. The Cooks took Jay and Fran under their wing, giving them the chance to share parties with the famous and the infamous that were making the scene in the budding swinging Sixties. But it was only at the more intimate dinners that Jay found the time and space to hold these notoriously restless beasts with tales of his spectacular failures in show business and show them that not all Americans were obsessed with success.

As curious a concept to the young blades that were tearing great holes in the fabric of English society with their satire and irreverence, as it was to Jay to live in a society where a hamburger was an alien idea.

Within a few months Jay and Fran had established a wide circle of friends (American-wise) and contacts that threatened to engulf them with a steady round of social activity. But he had received a shock when one of them, Jeremy Brooks, Literary Manager of the Royal Shakespeare Company, who he had asked to give him an opinion on a play he had written just before leaving the States, returned it with the comment: 'I expected something more outrageous from you.'

Considering the title was *Nobody Knows the Trouble I've Been* this was a shock to Jay's nervous system. Jay had never thought he had a sell-by date. Outrageous

To soothe his sense of injustice he reminded himself of what Chandler Brossard had written in an article entitled 'Reflections on my Beat Generation'.

> There is a Beat Generation manufactured by brazen, shameless academic hustlers... and another fabricated by the European remnants of the Children's Crusade... which involves a troupe of grinning, nudging bisexual scamps who juiced and doped heavily and bummed and slummed and thumbed rides to nirvana... In point of historical fact, the Beat Generation got their act together several years after a far less romantic, perhaps less huggable and certainly less publicised group of pioneers made their mark... Landesman was always very insightful, very ahead of everybody on the culture scene, and very encouraging. He was a gifted pioneer who influenced and freed a lot of talents. He was the first real radical in culture in my time. He was the originator and perpetrator of a lot of ideas and attitudes that permanently changed and charged the American cultural scene.

Still St Louis hadn't forgotten him and he became the 'Special Correspondent' for the *St Louis Post Dispatch* after he wrote a piece for them about 'The Biba Girls'. London certainly had enough erupting out of its underground to tease the sensibilities of anyone anywhere, not least the good drinkers of St Louis.

Jay's post from the States had convinced him that he had made the right move to leave. He had left behind the new phenomena of race riots, Barry Goldwater's bid to become president and the personal hang- ups of his friends who were taking everything from acid to analysis to deal with the disruptions to normal service. The best post script was from the man who had written Jay's Crystal Palace obit on his departure from St Louis: 'There isn't a decent place to get a drink in this town since you left.'

But Jay had found a decent place to get a drink in London. The Pickwick Club in Great Newport Street. A venue for attractive and louche people from various branches of the Arts and Entertainment world and slumming aristos looking for a bad reputation to go to bed with. Lively and creative conversation was on the menu as well as good food and live music.

Mischievous behaviour was inevitable so Jay was in his element. Princess Margaret and Lord Snowdon were sitting one night with a twittering bunch of friends at a table by the bar. One client had already been escorted to the door for pestering them, an actor known more for his drinking heroics than for his thespian abilities but that didn't faze Jay who was there with Fran and some friends.

'That man looks bored,' said Jay pointing at Lord Snowdon who indeed looked disenchanted. 'It's time some one tried to cheer him up.' And despite the protestations of Fran in particular he danced, or was it wove, his way to the royal table where he seemed to get an invitation to sit down. Lord Snowdon seemed quite pleased. After 10 minutes Jay returned to his own table and told the disbelieving friends that he had just been talking about the aviary Snowdon had designed for Regents Park and whose post modernist design had few defenders. 'Gave him architecture babble mixed with lots of approval. He loved it.'

He had barely finished telling the story when the maître d' came over to his table with a look that signalled intense disapproval, but saying 'His Lordship would like you to return to his table'.

There was a chorus of 'don't go 'and 'quit while you're ahead' but one American couldn't resist toasting Jay's chutzpah and that was enough to get him on his feet and back to the royal circle.

The return engagement lacked the spontaneity of the initial meeting and made worse because Jay tried to interest the bored royal with the story of his life. Even in an abridged form it proved too taxing for his Lordship. Jay had just learnt that royalty is only interested in one principle: 'if one allows a stranger to talk to one in a bar that conversation must be only about one.' But the only thing that bothered Jay was that he hadn't been introduced to the Princess Royal.

It is just a story – not to show off Jay's social credentials – but rather to illustrate the fact that he was able to look potential embarrassment in the eye and not flinch, even while all around him others were putting their heads in the sand or up their asses so as to avoid the situation Jay was deliberately putting himself in.

The only other person who was quite good at that was Mel Brooks, who joined up with Jay and Fran one night at the Pickwick as they had got to know each other through the Woody Allen connection. Unfortunately there is no record of them trying to out-do each other in this department. It would have been a joy to watch. In another life perhaps.

Next door to the Pickwick was the Kismet, an afternoon drinking club which was a host to a collection of Soho writers, artists, punters and brain damaged ex-Rank starlets whose past was their passport to getting pissed there. The favourite line when someone asked, 'What is that smell?' was the inevitable cry. 'Failure!' Jay met Christine Keeler there, who would become a friend of sorts of Fran who was still collecting failures for her lyrics.

But what Jay really enjoyed about it was that it was home to people, though often a generation younger, who were steeped in the life style of the 50s. They liked their jazz pure and their women not so pure and the women liked their men with a past more than those with a future. The truth was also that Jay had fallen head over heels in love with London. And he was sure that that love was reciprocated by one and all of the lovely people who lived in this great city.

By now he had found what would become the permanent home of the Landesmans, just a few houses down from their rented maisonette. This was a full Georgian house that until recently had been a light industrial business in Duncan Terrace. With the help from all and sundry they set about making the place habitable, with the final touches coming from Jay's eye as he scoured second hand shops, antique shops and skips for the artefacts that would add that distinctive look to Jay's World.

The time had come for both Jay and Fran to see whether they had any talent left to interest London town in the year 1965. Fran found an admirer and benefactor in Ned Sherrin and found herself working with John Barry, the Bond film composer to try write a title song for the film, *The Ipcress File.* Jay was asked by the West End producer, Michael Godron, to let him see his play: *Nobody Knows The Trouble I've Been,* as well as receiving a commission to write a one act play from the *St Louis Post Dispatch* for their bicentennial issue. More improbably, Peter Cook wanted him to take over a five minute slot he was doing for someone else's TV show.

The Landesman's had even been profiled by Hunter Davies for a *Sunday Times* feature where they had been characterised as an American 'Salinger type' family that had invaded London that previous spring. The migration of show business Americans to London was charging the scene with a lot of energy and the Landesmans were a part of that.

Norman Mailer came through their lives, promoting a new book and catching up with Jay who he had known from the mid 50s when he first became interested in hipsters and Beats and wrote his famous essay on the White Hipster. He had this vision of Jay as a kind of Jewish 'saint' who ensured that everyone was having a good time as well as giving him credit for being at the beginning of the Beat scene and helping to 'start it all.'

Around the same time Timothy Leary, another figure from their past, dropped in at Duncan Terrace. He was repaying a visit Jay and Fran had made to his Millbrook commune a couple of years earlier. Leary had encouraged Jay to take acid in the 'nose cone', a room in the tower of their great Victorian house equipped with special music, lighting and food for' space travelling'. After hours of waiting for lift-off, Leary couldn't account for Jay still being grounded, offering in the end to give him a booster shot of DMT. Jay poilitely declined but requested a couple of hits of Columbia Gold instead. As for the old mantra, Jay tuned in, turned on but then stood up and walked away, leaving Leary muttering about Jay being 'too transcendental'.

Leary was in town to hang out with R. D. Laing. Neither of these guys were to Jay's mind a bundle of laughs but at least Laing could relax with a Scotch and a joint and play great jazz on the piano. Laing and Landesman even danced together one night, as a heavy Zen party reduced Jay to a silence which was noticed by Laing. On asking him what the problem was Jay told him that 'I'm wearing my dancing shoes but nobody is dancing', whereupon Laing said: 'Well Jay. Let's dance then.'

Jay was pretty good at making even the most wired out intellectual find his frivolous self.

There were some though who were immune to his charms and chief among them were the Beatle Brethren, Paul McCartney and John Lennon, who he would meet in 1966 when they were trying to survive the mania they had created. He met them on separate occasions at Peter Cook's house and were memorable only for the ease with which one dismissed him as 'he's not a bad dancer for a guy his age' and the other preferred to build a castle from champagne glasses with Fran rather than engage in any repartee.

Needless to say, they hadn't a clue how to deal with a man who was enjoying life as an unembarrassed failure.

Well not exactly a failure. The Dublin Theatre Festival decided they wanted to do *Dearest Dracula,* a horror musical that jay had wanted to produce for some time with lyrics by Fran. Ten years before *The Rocky Horror Show* there was Jay's musical.

As the producer he was required to find an additional 10,000 dollars which he found with little trouble from backers in St Louis. Oh yes that city still had its uses. The show was an enthusiastic success in Dublin with superlatives like 'A production which for visual attack, stagecraft and all round excellence of singing, acting and dancing surpasses anything we have seen in Dublin in the field of musical comedy.'

Ah but the English critics had still to be heard from. And when they finally put down their pens you could hear *Dracula* cry with the pain of the stake that had been driven through its heart. Or maybe it was Jay's cry, who having had his spirits lifted with the early reviews found them plunging head first to the ground. Again. Remember *The Nervous Set?*

Or maybe it was the simple fact that musical comedy didn't pass through Dublin that often... like maybe once a millennium... so what did they know?

If Busby Berkeley hadn't come to London to give a talk at the opening of a season of his films at the National Film Society, *Dracula* would have remained that way. He had been one of the heroes of Jay's youth.

He arranged to interview him for one of his hot missives back to the *St Louis Post Dispatch* newspaper, and discovered that he was a very approachable guy. It suddenly occurred to Jay that he might like to work again (after years of shameful neglect) and so told Busby all about the romantic, dancing Irish *Dracula* experience and watched his eyes light up at the possibilities.

Jay was imagining what it would be like to be responsible for bringing Busby Berkeley back to Broadway with a dancing chorus of vampires and a tango-mad *Dracula*. Crazy idea of course but it would keep the investors from crying in their whiskies if he could continue to breath life into the blood sucking fiend.

He then contacted the horror meister himself, Vincent Price, who thought it was a great idea and asked to see the script. Busby was officially asked by Jay to stage and direct the show. As more money was needed to get the project running. Jay contacted the Broadway producer Ed Padula to come onboard. He was interested too. Everything was on go.

Busby Berkeley sent Jay a letter full of enthusiasm from Palm Springs where he lived, saying at the end of it: '...I firmly believe you have the capabilities, courage and determination to launch a most unusual and exciting show – and it would be a pleasure working with you...'

It would have been historic if it had worked... but the fates had other ideas.

Just as Jay was getting ready to go to New York for a meeting with all of them it began to unravel before his eyes. Padula, the producer was involved in a serious car accident. Price called saying that while he would love to do it. he was now booked for the next twoyears, leaving Busby dreaming of his comeback in Palm Springs but without the 'front money' Jay needed to get the show on the road.

Years later George Hamilton would play a prancing Dracula in the hit film *Love At First Bite* and Jay would think how timing was always just a deadly kiss away from making him immortal... My guess is that if Jay had had the success he craved, he probably would have died young.

But Fran's career was looking up. Her song 'The Ballad of the Sad Young Men' had been turned into a hit by Steve Lawrence, a well-known easy listening crooner of the time, and her New York publishers were on the phone to her trying to make up for their previous neglect.

Jay on the other hand was now determined to get off the treadmill of trying to 'make it'.

He defined success as the sweet taste of, but not the munching of the whole cake. His consolation was to feel that London was the right place to be a failure in.

'If I am doing nothing, I like to be doing nothing to some purpose That is what leisure means' (Alan Bennett)

London was not short of challenging amusements for the man who might have time on his hands and a good, relationship with his bank manager, based on a regular dollar stipend coming through from Fran's family in the States. Oh yes, that family, which Jay had so scandalised initially had finally come to admire their son-in-law's perverse but passionate take on life as well as realising that it kept their eccentric daughter as happy as a melancholic soul can be.

I realise that when I use the phrase' relationship with his bank manager', that in this 21st century of ours, this is terminology which would not be understood by a generation that has never had a bank manager, but only used electronic devices to communicate wishes to a computer. They don't know what they have missed. Second only in importance to the relationship you had with your male or female partner, your banker could be the bane or the salvation of your existence.

By 1967 Swinging London had become for many, Bewildering London.

London based reporters for international newspapers and particularly from America felt that London was on the road to perdition. Billy Graham thundered on his visits to Britain about the 'moral degeneration of English youth'. The British press and television were obsessed with the subject. But our ageing reporter on the scene and in the scene was in his element.

Wearing his first pair of plastic leather trousers courtesy of Carnaby Street, Jay had declared his house a refuge for the misunderstood and confused, and his living room became the playpen for friends from America, friends passing through Europe, friends of friends, friends from the night before and those who were looking for friends they had mislaid in the Landesman World. The atmosphere was of a passion play thinly disguised as a Feydeau farce.

People who made Jay laugh and who brought their own dope or were capable of challenging their lives were welcome to stick around. Others were asked, 'What are your plans?'

There was Pop Art and Pop Music to find, happenings to stumble over and art destruction to applaud. Other days were spent roving London on his 50cc Suzuki in search of material for his dispatches back to America. Jay was never short of a story. While others might see a sad sack or a frightening vision he saw the razor's edge slitting the jaded norms and pompous ways of a society trying to come to terms with what seemed like a campaign of terror.

But Jay needed projects like some people need a daily fix of liquorice. Not to feed you but to entertain you. So he was open to suggestions.

The Electric Garden was in the last stage of construction. This was to be a no-costs-spared disco in Convent Garden based on the Underground formula popular at the time, of mixed media. The problem was that the American City stockbroker whose baby this was, had not much of an idea what that entailed. He was going through a mid life crisis with a need to connect with the young scene but he also wanted it to be 'for grown ups'.

Enter Jay. Who told him that his only salvation was to hire one Jay Landesman as Artistic Director. His plan was to bring in the gallery and street performers and challenge them to perform to hundreds of people every night rather than just to the usual suspects found haunting their destructionist happenings. 'I can get you the kind of performers that know how to freak an audience out, but in the name of ART. That's what people want today,' Jay reassured the owner.

The club's name lent itself to easy word play and certainly was as hip as you could get. Here is a sample of one of Jay's press releases at the time:

Jay, Artistic Director of the Electric Garden, 1967
(photo Maurice Kaye, *Sun*).

Landesmania!

On Sunday 16 July, nine artists will present FUSED, an evening of shattering experiences. FUSED will include a Neon Ballet, spontaneous harangues (four speakers from Hyde Park), visual dialogues based on recently discovered medieval texts, electronic confessions, surprise sound machines and hate-waves based on audience paranoia plus visual trickery incorporating non musical instruments...

The media headlines were delightful: 'Pop Underground Surfaces in West End', 'Covent Garden Goes Electric' and the BBC turned up on the opening night to record the event.

By the end of the night Jay was once again a 'street genius' and there was a lot of talk about love and life liberated by art. Yeah, Yeah...the tills were happy and happy tills made Jay popular.

The 'real' underground's mouthpiece, the *International Times*, were rather less pleased to find 'their' people hijacked by this 'promoter' of the alternative life style with his bouncers at the door. It wasn't Jay's idea, but the Mad Millionaire Mid-Lifer from Manhattan, but it was he who got fingered.

Things came to a head, as they do when you are dealing with combustible elements, the night Yoko Ono debuted at the Electric Garden. This was when she had yet to become the little Ying to John Lennon's mighty Yang. She was trying out her own version of mass communication, by sitting on a platform, bound in surgical tape and inviting people to cut little pieces from it while she howled like a Japanese wolverine in heat.

Some were quite taken by her attempt to share her love for the world. The majority, which included the management but not Jay, who encouraged her to keep screaming, found the cacaphony unbearable and a riot soon blossomed.

The end result was that Yoko and her then husband, Tony Cox, were manhandled out of the club, Jay was fired but then reinstated at dawn, and the *International Times* snarled:

[93]

What the fuck is happening on the scene?... there are bad, evil vibrations with the scene, which, if not blocked, may just blow the whole thing apart... the explosion at the Electric Garden exposed a group of hard cash-gangsters whose sole intention is to exploit known artists on the scene and yourself, the audience. How did this come about? Who scored? Wake up Jay Landesman, you're the connection.

Yoke was rather more forgiving, as was her nature...' Let's not throw bad vibrations at each other. Let's all be beautiful together. Let's.

The lights went out at the Electric Garden soon after. Reconnected as Middle Earth, without the art and without the stockbroker, but with a new artistic director, it became the born-again headquarters of the Underground and a big success.

Jay's 'projectus interruptus' was scoring one hundred percent.

'*If at first you don't succeed, try, try again
Then quit. No use being a damn fool about
it*' (*W.C.Fields*)

'You've come just in time. I'm going through a very social phase.'
That was Jay welcoming his old friend John Clellon Holmes to Islington in 1988.

As mentioned before, La Casa Landesman had become a cara-
vanserai for the performers and shakers, particularly the Americans
who he might have booked back at the Crystal Palace or who never
were graced with a booking but had somehow got their fame without his assistance.

After a series of nights which would have made a fly flinch if it
had been on the wall documenting their excesses, and visits to the
King's Road, Jim Haynes's Arts Lab, the Roundhouse Theatre, the
Playboy Club and Jay's martini haunts he found his friend less than
convinced about the life style Jay was enjoying. Everything seemed
like a déjà vu experience for him. It wasn't until years later that Jay
understood that Holmes didn't have his ability to keep re-invent-
ing himself and carrying on as if the next wave was as good as the
last and look forward to the next. Holmes had found the period
he loved, the late 40s and early 50s and was getting gloomier-and
angrier-at-the turn of social and cultural events in America and by
extension in England. Holmes was homesick for 'the old country'
and 'the old ways'. He couldn't laugh at it all as he once would have
done.

But this was exactly the talent that Jay had. It was a time of great
frivolity and uncomplicated wickedness and he absorbed none of
the more political or destructive anarchy that was part of the 'make
love, not war' challenges.

But Holmes had made him think. He had been described in
Holmes's book *Nothing More To Declare* as one of the 'representa-

[95]

tive men' of his generation along with Ginsberg, Kerouac and Leg-man.

Holmes had written '... Landesman possessed, years before it was chic or marketable, what would now be called the Pop imagination... for any and all evidences of a unique and unconventional point of view interested him, and he looked for this evidence in junk shops, movie houses and news-stands, as well as in bookstores, art galleries and theatres... he represented a side of my generation and its experiences: the game playing, style enamoured, pomposity puncturing side. The funny, hip, mordant, nosy, meaningful-side... everything he did had an aura of elaborate burlesque about it...'

So what was his role to be as he approached his 50th birthday, in those 'interesting times'.

He made a stab at returning to the antiques business, with some degree of success, in Camden Passage, but found himself on the losing end of a partnership based more on good taste than business acumen. As Fran said: 'Face it Jay, you're a disgrace to your heritage. Whoever heard of a dumb Jewish businessman?'

He was finding that people were putting him up against the agent provocateurs of the time as if to measure their championship potential. He felt that he was getting used as a sparring partner.

Nathan Silver, a fellow American and world renowned architecture expert, paired him up with George Steiner, the philosopher, one evening to find the 'dramatic contrasts between people on a social level' and expected a confrontation of types. But Jay and Steiner enjoyed musings on the decline of the West which foiled this plan.

The same happened when the young and outrageous Germaine Greer came on the scene and appeared at another of Silver's dinners. Jay got along well with her, not least because of his unique relationship to Fran, but also because Jay just was not a man for the grandstanding 'confrontation'.

After almost six years in London, by 1970 the old pattern of 'too many parties, too many pals' experience in New York re-emerged.

The hippy culture had given way to political activism and in many cases to disillusionment with the state of play. In the middle of this Jay found his own enlightenment. He had locked into what would become one of the major issues of the Western Hemisphere in the years to come. Diet. More specifically, the food that would change the way we thought about ourselves and the environment. Macrobiotics.

A whole new life began; it revolved around food.

He had tuned into this esoteric (as it was at the time) concept after sharing a visit to Stonehenge with a group of off-the-wall characters who were going to celebrate the summer solstice. These were the days when you could dance in the circle and hug the stones. A fellow called Jordan Reynolds convinced Jay that the truth of ones life was to be found in the body and this could be released or triggered by the type of food one consumed. Jay was converted.

The headlines should have read: Macrobiotic Missionary found by ex-Martini Man.

Jay did all the shopping and some of the cooking. He got so carried away with his new philosophy that he accepted becoming a cog in a miniature macrobiotic empire started by the teenage entrepreneurs Gregory and Craig Sams. They started with a macrobiotic restaurant, progressed to a natural food store and eventually a wholesale distribution company that would become the Whole Earth brand.

As natural foods were almost unheard of in those days, Jay became their salesman and public relations expert, writing features on the glories of brown rice and the joys of seaweed. He even squeezed out a sexual angle to it by describing its potency-enhancing properties and selling the story to the top soft porn magazine of the time.

In health food circles he was known as 'Stan Stunning', the Johnny Appleseed of the natural foods movement. He had his picture taken with Barbara Cartland, dressed in a jacket made of old rice sacks (with the yin-yang symbol on the back), showing her a package of their product. Cartland had already been a long time devotee of health foods.

The *Sunday Times* was invited over for dinner with the Landesman family which resulted in a feature on the 'ideal macro family'.

'It's very marriage building,' said Fran with a curious mixture of hope and tongue in cheek. 'Life has become simple and loving...'

Jay's friends were less enthusiastic. Those brave enough to accept an invitation for dinner stayed for the miso soup but left before the lectures. While their scepticism was no surprise, considering the lifestyles they had all once shared, to Jay, this conversion had allowed him to find a bit of meaning in a world that was gradually losing its faith in anything other than obsessive 'liberation'. He felt that the discipline necessary to abandon previous bad habits was a life that held great benefits to the lost souls of the sixties. As he wrote in OZ magazine 'The real revolution begins right under your nose – open your mouth and chew!'

Oh Yes.. Jay had become a born-again nutritional fundamentalist. His social circle was still wide though some were leery of this Duncan Terrace prophet that had sprung from their midst. The word spread through the entertainment world and he found converts. His most successful one was the musician Paul Jones who would 'immortalise' Jay and Fran in his song 'Stan Stunning and The Noodle Queen'.

But it didn't last. Does that sound familiar by now?

You could blame it this time on his genetic makeup or on the wicked insistence of his meat loving friends who had never given up hope that he would return to the world he knew best or on the fact that getting involved in politics, even about food, brought him out in a terrible rash. Whatever.

The whole food business became an ideological battleground between the American and English apostles to the cause which left Jay with a need to check up on his state of mind, and those of his family with Robin Skynner, who would eventually collaborate with John Cleese on the book *Families and How to Survive Them*.

Jay (right) with Barbara Cartland and Gregory Sams.

His final words to them were: 'You're Hansel and Gretel walking in the woods, holding hands like children. You refuse to grow up.'

Fran and Jay felt that this was reassuring news. There is no record of what their two children thought of that.

And so they returned to their hedonistic ways... just in time for Jay to be able to accept an invitation from Jim Haynes to join a distinguished crowd as a juror at the Wet Dream Festival in Amsterdam. As every jury member had to provide a nude photograph of themselves, it goes without saying that Jay felt mighty comfortable with this event, which featured hard and soft core films, performing artists, parties, workshops, seminars and orgies.

Jay had skipped from the Health Food Revolution to the Sexual Revolution without a great deal of angst. It was just another station on the Landesman Railway which ran on his cultural fun conduit all the way to the horizon without a break.

About this time he met another master prankster and fun lover, Ken Kesey. He was in London promoting *The Electric Kool-Aid Acid Test*, a book written by Tom Wolfe, about Kesey's adventures on a psychedelic bus trip around the States with a bunch of eccentric jokers, trying to turn America on. Which he certainly did with the university crowd at the time.

They had an organic food but also an orgasmic approach to life that made them comfortable buddies though it was hard to tell who was most capable of letting their obsessions rule their lives. But Kesey had to return home, having to abandon a documentary he wanted to make with Jay's help which would have had the Hells Angels and the Druids in a crazed new age relationship based around Stonehenge.

But he had left Jay with a thought. Several actually.

Jay was an American who had never really thought about what that meant. He had been born in an intoxicatingly free playground with all the toys you could buy to be happy in a capitalist sand box. Now the world was taking against America. For its involvement in the Vietnam war. For its race riots. Supporting its campus demonstrations. Against President Nixon. There was an anti-American sentiment in the air. And he was not happy with this state of affairs It grated on him in a way that wasn't obvious but it was getting on his nerves. After all, that was the country he wanted as his last resting place – in spite of Fran saying: 'Are you kidding? That sounds like a lot of work. Forget it.'

Yet this was the country that Jay had mercilessly satirised, whose hypocrisy he had challenged, whose outcasts he had championed and whose society he had fled. To become an American Abroad. Not an Ugly American but a Loveable Affable Roguish American. Something like an American in Paris circa 1930. But it was now 1974.

The Art Deco bus in Cannes.

It was time for a little break and fresh air. When the opportunity came up to buy a vintage Art Deco bus, he took it.

It was time to try a slice of Life on the Road.

First of all Jay and Fran tried out a few French lessons to see if they could get their creative arts around a foreign language. They couldn't. Fran managed one phrase which was probably only wish fulfilment: 'Le chien a mangé mon mari', while Jay mastered in perfect French, 'the soles of my shoes have holes' which was his way, I imagine, of carrying at least one social ice-breaker to France.

They had decided to take their bus down to the Cannes Film Festival. Not much is known of the road they took or the adventures along the way but they must have looked like two kids skipping school and acted like a couple of accidental tourists from another planet.

It was the year that Cannes discovered alternative cinema and a new school of directors. The avant-garde work of yesteryear had become erotic/political feature movies as the film industry tried to exploit the student and the sexual revolution.

Once the bus was strategically parked so that it could be both admired and yet afford them some privacy. Jay and Fran started receiving guests. After three days they barely had space for themselves as some of the guests made it their alternative home, even though some of them were staying in the best hotels in Cannes. Film critics and directors, actors and actresses... some whose name lasted a season and others whose names can still be dropped with a satisfying thud... The bus is where they came for tea and post-mortems on the previous nights indiscretions, or for martinis and a joint to relax after a night dodging the paparazzi.

But Jay and Fran were exhausted by it. Surrounded by a language they couldn't communicate in and funny cultural habits that were no longer jokey. And worst of all for Jay, knowing with profound conviction that his whole persona would get lost in translation.

While others might have thought that this should have been a prelude to hitting the high road to Katmandu, Jay's 55 year old senses told him that it was a better idea to return to London with their 'Cannescapade 'ready for dinner and cocktail chit chat at Duncan Terrace.

Fran and Jay may have been Far Out but they would not be going Out That Far again.

In any case there were entertainments closer to home, like the visit by the American cellist Charlotte Moorman who was famous for her annual parade of 'avant-garde' happenings in New York. Her husband, who was an engineering genius, had designed the world's first television bra especially for the full bosomed Charlotte. It featured two miniature television sets which could present *News at Ten* and a BBC documentary simultaneously. As Charlotte and husband were house guests of the Landesmans, it goes without saying that Jay was involved as a producer for the event in his living room, as it was repeatedly tested, as well as an enthusiastic audience member on the night of her performance in London where for an encore, she turned her breasts to the audience and replayed their stunned reaction on her twin sets. The caption to the *Daily Mirror*'s picture was 'A Girl with Two Points of View'.

Charlotte Moorman was able to top this at a topless performance at the Roundhouse the following week, where she played an entire Saint-Saens concerto on a cello made of ice with a glass bow before the cello melted. Although she got frost bite on one breast, the evening was another successful chapter for this pioneering video and performance artist. The music wasn't bad either.

'It is better to be a has-been than a never-was' (Cecil Parkinson)

One day John Steinbeck Junior walked into Jay's life. He arrived at Jay's doorstep as a friend of a friend of Jay's and proceeded to make himself at home in Duncan Terrace, parking himself in the spare room. It didn't take long for Jay to realise this fella was not going to leave in a hurry, so they settled down to a pleasant routine of afternoon drinking sessions and evening project planning.

They were both about the same age, with what little seniority there was, going Jay's way. Inevitably the projects tended to be about how that famous name could be properly exploited. Fran wrote a wry and insightful poem about John Jr. that summed up the burden of carrying a famous name:

> The people ask you questions about your father's life
> His habits and his pastimes, his crazy second wife
> You answer them with patience, supply the missing link
> The only thing you ask them is buy another drink...'

They ended up forming an agency for seriously flawed writers, actors and artists. They called it Creative Arts Liberated. It was dedicated to liberating the artist from becoming depressed about having the talent, but not the competitive spirit. Their motto was: We take the sting out of success and put the fun back in failure.'

There was a certain Zen zing to this which appealed to the Buddhist in Steinbeck Junior and certainly to the creative swings and roundabouts of Jay Landesman's career.

It might be fair to say at this point, that if Jay was the ringmaster of a circus, then it was one from which all the animals had fled, barring a curious rodent or two, the performers had vanished to other venues, the accountant had eloped with the last musician and the ticket lady was muttering crazily to herself as she counted out invisible tickets to invisible patrons... but that didn't mean that Jay wasn't still out there cracking his whip to the tune of 'There's always tomorrow...'

The fun lasted until Steinbeck ended up going to India with a lady he had fallen in love with, the writer Rosie Boycott, on a motorbike to help a dying friend find a miracle working guru. A fitting end and in the right spirit for a doomed enterprise.

But Jay was still in business, after a fashion. He had one client on his books that he felt he had to put some serious energy into. Fran Landesman.

Her career had taken a strange turn. She had been invited to read some of her poetry at a special event in the crypt of St-Martin-in-the-Fields. She had had her doubts about reading her rhymed poems at a time when free verse was all the rage, but to her surprise she got a rousing reception from a receptive audience which included many of the hard bitten poets of the day. She had now developed a cool, self deprecating charm that went hand in glove with her wry observations of desperate conversations in smart bars or brooded about in lonely rooms.

Jay decided to put a number of the poems and lyrics into print and managed to do the job with professional values. This would be his first foray into publishing since the days of *Neurotica*. The book was called *The Ballad of the Sad Young Men and Other Verse* and it was a Landesman success. Jay was a publisher again.

Wth her reputation firmly established, Jay found it easy to get her gigs at arts centres, jazz festivals, universities and theatre clubs all over England. She was now CAL's only client who needed all of Jay's attention so he slipped into the role of her personal manager.

But it wasn't easy for our limelighting friend to have to take that step-back role. To become Fran's husband, Jay, after a lifetime of her being Jay's wife, Fran, demanded a humility that was not exactly in his nature. He had to forget his past or find a new project for himself.

Sure enough, an oddball character walked into his life with the requisite formula of light reef This was Gary Davis, the original architect of World Citizenship, an organisation dedicated to challenging the concept of nations and nationality by making everybody a Citizen of the World.

Once a USAF bomber pilot. He had made himself world famous, shortly after the Second cld War, by tearing up his American passport on the steps of the United States Congress in front of news reel cameras and declaring himself World Citizen Number One. Since then he had travelled round the world promoting his quixotic vision of a united world party.

That such a man should land on Jay's doorstep should surprise no one. But what did surprise Jay was that he was offered the position as the party's Ambassador to the Court of St James. His house was to become the diplomatic headquarters for the party.

Needless to say, this was to become a media event. Thames Television was there to record the occasion. With the World Flag tied to a mop handle outside the bedroom window, Jay and Fran were interviewed in the doorway of their new diplomatic residence. When Jay was asked about his qualifications for this high office he had no problem finding the appropriate response: 'I have all the right clothes necessary to fulfil the appointment.'

And on being asked 'Who is the lovely lady?' Jay put his arm around the still stunned Fran and said 'This is my Ambassadorable, of course.'

Though the ceremony and interview were broadcast on the evening news that summer night, Jay never made it to the Court of St James. Invitation lost in the post no doubt. Unfortunately an oversight that was never rectified and by the time autumn arrived, the carnival had moved on to Switzerland and the passport division of the World Citizenship Party had been taken over by true believers. Leaving Jay with another memory of how sweet the limelight tastes.

Gary Davis at the diplomatic headquarters of World Citizenship,
1960
(photo *Daily Mirror*).

'The man who works and is not bored is never old' (Pablo Casals)

As you may have noticed so far, Jay was not into physical heroics. But he was partial to heroic endeavours if it meant that people could enjoy a slice of life, produced by him, that would give them fresh insights into themselves and their social environment.

Jay had met Elisabeth Smart the first week he had arrived in London and had remained an ardent admirer of her poetry ever since. He was one of the 300 guests that had attended the paperback launch of *By Grand Central Station I Sat Down and Wept* at the Roundhouse in 1966. But since those heady days, she had been living in obscurity in a remote part of Suffolk cultivating her garden and suffering a classic case of writer's block. This, in spite of the fact that the book at become a major underground classic.

Apparently one of the contributing factors to her block and disappearance was that she didn't have a sympathetic publisher to encourage her. A mutual friend of both of them was the writer Jill Neville, who suggested that Jay could be the perfect man for this delicate task, especially now that he had started publishing again: 'You two would make a perfect team' was her verdict.

So they met at the French House in Soho, their mutual drinking den. And hit it off just fine, though it was clear that she knew more about publishing than he did as she suggested what sort of contracts might be appropriate for the various rights involved.

Encouraged by her trust in him and lusting for creative action, Jay threw himself into the project with all his talents at full throttle, deciding that producing a book and promoting an author weren't that different from producing a show.

So he went on personal visits to all the booksellers, distributors and bookshop owners to tell them that Elisabeth Smart was on the comeback trail with a new book of poems entitled *A Bonus*. He rallied all the friends he had made in the media during his years in London to help bring in a hit. On the day the book came out, many of her admirers in the literary world followed up with interviews and reviews which gave Elisabeth's work the attention she deserved. It was considered a success and a best seller as far as poetry is able to go down that road.

Jay thought it was time to re-issue *Grand Central Station* in hardback. When he suggested that she might want a more serious publisher for this, her reply was: 'No. You do it. I like the way you get things done without a fuss. I have another book I just finished that you can have too.'

To say Jay was flattered would be underestimating his reaction. A money-making project to boot made it all bliss.

The relationship between publisher and writer flourished, nourished by constant consultations on what was happening and outlining future projects together. Press interviews and public readings were anathema to her but with Jay's encouragement she performed like a veteran. The cream on the cake arrived when the *Observer* gave her the Literary Comeback of the Year award for 1977.

Fly in the ointment anywhere? Unfortunately yes. Elisabeth's new novel *The Assumption of the Rogues and Rascals* proved to be a difficult read and the literary establishment were less than kind to something they could not understand. In spite of the poor reviews, she was in demand. But it was *Grand Central* that was keeping her in the public eye. To such a degree that a film company wanted an option to make it into a feature film.

Well here is where Jay's talents failed to keep pace with his ambitions and failed to handle the negotiations to Elisabeth's satisfaction. She resented his encouraging her on the whole film project, accusing him of conspiring to invade her privacy. Saying, as many have said before her and since: 'I sold them the rights to my book, not to my life.'

In spite of all the encouragement she received from friends and admirers, Elisabeth Smart would write no more, returning to her solitary country life, drifting away from Jay and wondering whether she should write her autobiography.

Jay didn't bother holding his breath over that one, feeling that he had been expelled from her inner circle for being a tad too smart for his own good. His role was over and his 'Smart' innings finished. Fading understanding would probably be given as the cause.

≈•

Jay was 58 years old. Some would call it a time to think of retiring. He was however now doing something he was good at and most importantly was having fun doing it too. Now that he was a real publisher it was time to get a real office.

That was found in Soho, on Wardour street, adjacent to a sex cinema called Spankorama, where Jay could find some light relief with suitable friends if the afternoons were a little quiet.

His working pattern began to emerge. It was a style of publishing not then common or practised by any of the established houses which was to get the books out fast, with small advances and big promises, maximising the promotion of the book and himself. Discovering writers was exciting but what really gave Jay his adrenaline rush was the promotion.

First among his new clients was Heathcote Williams with his manuscript for *Hancock's Last Half Hour*. Heathcote loved the idea that Jay would publicise his lurid and flamboyant past exploits which ran the gamut from wild happenings, plays like *AC/DC* and *The Speakers*, orgiastic musicals and creating the Ruff Tuff Cream Puff Estate Agency which provided free accommodation for the homeless to his involvement with saving whales and dolphins before they had become universal causes.

The bible of the industry, *The Bookseller*, was so intrigued by his operation that they asked him to write up his experiences for the

magazine. Thus began a series of occasional articles on the trials
and tribulations of being a small publisher which gave Jay a national
recognition that advertising couldn't buy. It put a sense of fun into
what was still a very straight laced business.

What appealed to him most was getting a book out of someone
who had never thought of writing one. 'Everyone has a story' was his
mantra. Everyone was a potential prospect and his by now regular
watering hole, The French Pub on Dean Street, was where he went
to hunt for his hopefuls. Another publisher doing much the same
was Peter Owen and a kind of competition developed between them
as they surveyed the talent available from opposite sides of the bar.

In the course of duty Jay had to supply a fair amount of drink
to the assembly, trying to distinguish between the genuine nugget
and fool's gold. Many an afternoon's trawling might end up with a
golden handshake that by the following day would have beentrans-
formed into just another dirty hand. I imagine that was covered as
genuine business expenses though.

One of Jay's surprise discoveries was a fourteen year old kid called
Gideon Sams, son of Craig Sams, who he had worked with during
his macrobiotic days. Gideon's mother had found a school project
he had written and intrigued by its contents showed it to Jay who
immediately saw its potential. It was a short account of the newly
developing punk scene.

To publish the world's first punk novel would be a coup and he
felt sure that it would upset the publishing trade enough that there
would sufficient publicity to make it commercially viable. Gideon
had basically written the *Romeo and Juliet* story in punk language
and set it in the world he observed in his own school yard. Jay saw
there was enough immediacy and violence to satisfy anyone's interest in the punk movement.

Jay had the book out in three weeks after getting the school
project fattened up to a decent 62-page manuscript. The cover featured a Johnny Rotten clone with a real, life size safety pin through
his nose.

Interviews and features appeared in everything from the *Melody Maker* to the *Sunday Times* and *Observer*. Gideon played his part and Jay made sure the part was on the money. The book was a commercial success everywhere except in America where they thought it was too violent. It does seem to be an inscrutable mystery to the rest of the world that a country with a gun-worshiping culture like the United States, can still find itself fearing violence in the written word.

But Jay was about to move from the overtly provocative to more prosaic pastures.

He had been warned that books about libraries were death traps. Well, that wasn't a closely guarded secret but he felt there might be an angle he could find on this truism. He saw a letter in the National Book League's newsletter from a librarian who identified himself as Barry Bowles, Punk Correspondent of the *New Library World*, and who went on to describe himself as: 'a resident lecturer in frustration at north London bus stops. In 1963 headed south for loneliness and libraries, where in 15 short years rose from assistant librarian to older assistant... meantime *Ambit* published his poetry at the insistence of London Transport to avoid a body on the track... and as Captain Lust entertains the gentlemen with stones in *Penthouse* magazine, *Men Only* and *Knave*.'

A novel surfaced from their collaboration. *Between the Stacks*. A sassy and funny tale of the everyday adventures of a librarian as she 'womans' her post somewhere in the big city. Jay had badges made that said 'Get it Between the Stacks' and sent them to all the librarians in the land.

Libraries bought copies by the shelf load. Librarians were more discreet and the public was mildly interested.

What was far more important was that Jay's reputation as an original publisher was growing. The range of subjects, the unconventional promotional drive behind them, amused and impressed the trade and the public. It was also reassuring to the other publishers that there was still room for a maverick in their business.

But there was a sense that he now had to get himself sorted out as a company. He was in a halfway house between being a serious publishing company and an eccentric and quixotic enterprise which was the basis of its reputation. One thing that was not under threat was the sense of bon viveur hedonism that permeated the offices in Soho. Small parties organised at the drop of a hat to celebrate successes and afternoon delights just for the hell of it, made the offices of Jay Landesman, Publisher, a popular destination for those who could give them good publicity and those who were simply good company. Even after the booze ran out.

By now Jay had hired a stunning long-legged rebel by the name of Pamela Hardyment, who, while happy to star during party time also had a serious side to her that made Jay work a little harder to get his production values right and pay attention to new technology. Romantic conversations over a drink at the end of the day turned into printing seminars with Pamela making more sense than him.

Jay's credibility in the world of punk wouldn't have been complete if he hadn't met its most notorious citizen at the time. Did I say citizen...? I think I meant professional irritant.

That of course was the master needler and dyspeptic, Johnny Rotten. And where else to meet him but at Jay's traditional New Year's Day party. This was the sort of party you did not go to if you were trying to recover from a new Year's Eve hangover, It was the party that encouraged people to show off their New Year's resolutions and flaunt the new friends they had found in the dog hours of the old year.

That must have been how Rotten found himself guided into Fran's room, where seduced by a very expensive scotch provided by Jay, he was recited to by Fran who had just witten a poem about him:

> ... We know you're gonna make it
> But maybe it's too late If by the time you make it

You're what you used to hate
You'll end up fat and frightened
And cut off like the King
With yes men to protect you
And nothing left to sing.

Mr Rotten, why be a hit?
When you're Top of the Pops
Then you're right in the shit
They'll process your protest
And fuck up your view
They're gonna make a sausage out of you...

Rotten little Johnny was not best pleased to hear of himself selling down the river when he had hardly started with the spitting he had in mind: 'It's going to give me great pleasure to prove you wrong,' he snarled as he stamped out of the house into a sunny afternoon, which must have alarmed him, as he wouldn't have had a chance to notice it in Fran's den.

When Johnny R. became plain John Lydon he must have thought he had got the better of anyone predicting anything about him. So there. But generally speaking, Fran was the one with a decent claim to entertainment fame. Not without Jay's promotional support, that is true, and he made it possible to tie in the publication of her second book by Cape with a two-week appearance at Ronnie Scott's. She shared the bill with Dexter Gordon, the great saxophonist and by the end of her stint, the jazz cognoscenti had given the performance their approval. She also discovered that Tom Waits, who had got to know them through his love of the Beats, was one of her admirers.

But her turning point was the Edinburgh Festival in 1980. Despite landing in an out of the way venue, Jay had played the part of a crazed carnival barker out in the street, inviting people to 'step inside folks and see the best show in town. The tough little lady direct from New York...' And it had worked. For the first time she had a taste of what it was like to be accepted unconditionally by students, punks and middle-aged mums. She definitely was Someone now and about time too.

As far as Jay was concerned, this meant that they both had lives to lead without one feeling that the other was locked in a cage and needing attention feeding. Talking of which, Fran had this line for Jay: 'I married you for better or worse, but not for lunch.'

Sally Vincent, who was doing an article for the *Observer* on unconventional lives within the framework of a conventional marriage had this to say about the Landesman household:

> All this talk about Having Fun, as though it was nothing to be ashamed of, is enough to make you nervous of what might be expected of you. But there is a real coal fire in the grate and the cat is laundering herself in front of it, somebody is strumming a guitar and what you mostly feel here is cared for... Like the fabric of their home, the Landesman life is either a terrible mess in need of major repair and a good clean up, or it's eccentrically, humanely, bravely and infinitely generously disposed... 'Suburban Swingers,' Jay says, relaxed as spaghetti, but bordering on scornful, 'always abuse the thing they take to be their freedom. They go about having fun like they were boy scouts on a mission. They can't have a simple little affair without sighing about running away together like what they are really doing is trying to find a way out of their misery. So they play all those sad games where they throw their keys into a heap and then oblige each other to fornicate with whoever picks them up. They don't even take any responsibility for what they are up to.

Jay was a youthful looking 61-year-old with a voice to liberate the libidos of young ladies and a personality pitched rakishly to catch them. Little about him had changed from his naughty days in the

50s. All that had changed was that he was still misbehaving in the 1980s.

Who needed a portrait painted by an artist up in the attic when you could have a portrait painted by a poet encouraging you to be Dorian Grey:

> Don't change.
> Stay the way you are.
> Don't change.
> You were always a star.
>
> It's marvellous to see you coming,
> Arrayed in splendour, cheerng up the street,
> A Jewish prince who's done a little slumming,
> Like Fred Astaire, you never miss a beat.
>
> Don't leave.
> For the world that's so wide
> I'd grieve
> Without you by my side.
>
> Time marches on but you are still dancing,
> Still trying to extend your range.
> Technology may keep advancing
> And things and people grow more strange,
> But please don't go too far.
>
> Just stay the way you are.
> Don't change!

Needless to say Jay was intending to do just that.

'A living dog is better than a dead lion' (The Bible)

By 1980 Jay had a collection of writers unsurpassed for eccentricity who were heroic drinkers and no strangers to failure. The Colony Room was a drinking club that collected quite a few of these Soho yeomen and here was where he got together with Dan Farson, a journalist and writer, to concoct a cunning satire on the major political story of the day. The Jeremy Thorpe trial.

In order to avoid libel, Farson told the story from a dog's point of view, with all the dogs based on the real life characters. Farson was a quick writer and Jay was a fast publisher so they managed to get it all finished to coincide with the end of the trial. The tale concluded with an assumption of Thorpe's guilt and the book, *The Dog Who Knew Too Much*, was published on the day of the verdict – which, unfortunately for them was – not guilty.

However the book was well received by the critics. George Melly, in the *New Society*, concluded that: 'Long after the exact events it parallels have faded from memory, *The Dog Who Knew Too Much*, will survive on its own merits. The mark of first class satire is that it has a universal as well as a contemporary point...this book passes that test.'

Encouraging reviews but not a noticeable seller. But Jay must have thought the dog theme had more mileage left to it because he soon found himself accepting a manuscript of the world's first cookbook devoted to canine gastronomy, using food appealing to both man and beast, *The Good Dog's Cookbook* by Richard Graham.

The writer was an authority on food and wine, contributing articles to *The Times* and *The Good Food Guide* as well, obviously, as being a passionate lover of dogs.

With clever illustrations and funny quotes from well known dog owners like Elaine Stritch ('My dog loved this book so much she ate it')and Jilly Cooper ('It is a must for all four stockings this Christmas') on the cover, the book earned that choice position next to the till in many bookshops across the country. It was a goer.

As always sales were helped along with stunts to maximise publicity. To coincide with the London Book Fair, Jay got a *Sun* newspaper reporter to attend a 'canine party' in Chelsea which was described, with tongue firmly in cheek, as if it was a celebrity dinner occasion.

Knowing of Christina Foyle's love of dogs, Jay sent her a special copy of the book which resulted in his getting a much sought-after front window display at Foyle's Bookshop.

All in all he thought that he now had a book he could make a killing on, so he decided to take a small booth at the Frankfurt Book Fair where world rights are bought and sold. This was a major testing ground and it proved to be fertile ground. It was enlivened by Jay parading through the halls being led by a huge Pyrenean mountain dog while wearing a chefs hat. The Japanese in particular were very keen to get the rights, though perhaps through a temporary misunderstanding by the Japanese publisher, who thought it was a book about how to cook dogs... I am sure that Jay would not have discouraged the thought if he was going to get the deal... 'Whatever turns you on in the land of the Rising Sun is fine by me'.

The same writer carne up with another book about cuisine for cats which proved to be even more popular than the dog cookbook, proving once and for all that Britain is a feline- more than a canine-loving country. Not withstanding, a further book did come out called *The Good Dog's Guide to Better Living* which incorporated ideas for careers for the ambitious canine, good dog etiquette and essentials for a dog's education.

It was a dog's life for Jay and that success made him go all chancey again. His next venture would be a biography of an ex-communist homosexual, lapsed Catholic poet with a drinking problem. Eddie Linden had started a magazine called *Aquarius* with a capital investment of £4 in 1970 and while he hustled friends and the Arts Council for money to keep it going, he supported himself by charring for his better known and successful peers, getting to be known as the 'Butler to Literature'.

This was a story straight from the Jay Landesman cannon of failures that deserved some kind of recognition. The jacket had quotes from many of his famous friends, including Harold Pinter, Peter Porter, Brian Patten and John Montague. The book itself, *Who is Eddie Linden?* was written by Sebastian Barker, who had known Eddie all his life.

The book almost sold out its first printing, with Jay having suggested that Eddie take review copies of the book in person to likely literary editors, not only in England but also to Scotland and Ireland. The reviews were good and came from a wide spectrum of publications. The world saw him as a poor man's Quentin Crisp. Eddie saw himself on the verge of vindication... but it was not to be.

The truth was that in Thatcher's world, people were more interested in the triumph of bastards than the triumph of a small soul's survival. He got his fifteen minutes in the spotlight but Jay couldn't make him bankable.

There would be further triumphs for Jay. Fran had become most high profile as she was featured time and again in slick women's magazines by a young generation that understood the spirit in which she wrote and admired the lifestyle that had generated her experiences. Jay published her third volume of verse, *More Truth than Poetry*.

It was Jay's oldest son, Cosmo, now an ambitious 27-year-old with a solid grounding in literary bric-a-brac who suggested publishing the best of the 'High Life' and 'Low Life' columns from the *Spectator* magazine.

High Life, Low Life was greeted warmly by the media. After all, the writers Jeffrey Bernard and Taki were the icons of their particular sets. Bernard, of the Soho led crowd of artists and writers and drinkers, and Taki, the Greek millionaire, of the aspiring and upper class tendencies that liked his raffish take on them. Auberon Waugh was moved to write that 'They have more to say about contemporary society than Gibbon in his *Decline and Fall of the Roman Empire*.'

Everyone made money on this one even though Taki was hardly in need of any extra folding money. It was the thought that counts, I imagine. But it did make a big difference to Jeffrey Bernard, as after this, he found himself with a higher profile lifestyle and able to generate more income for his vodka-fuelled excesses.

It was a long road from the distant shore of *Neurotica* but while then he wanted to poke society's eye, now he was just interested n tickling its funny bone if he could. By now Jay's reputation was such that he could have commissioned a book on just about anything oddball, off-the-wall or plain delirious and expect it to have a life of its own if he published it.

But instead he chose the path of titillation. He decided to publish a scholarly bibliography of the collection of erotica in the British Library, which they kept locked up, away from the public eye. The author of what would be called *The Private Case*, was a picture editor by profession, Patrick J. Kearney, who managed to convince the Museum to let him catalogue the complete collection.

The potential market for such a bibliography was limited to reference libraries, antiquarian booksellers and serious collectors of erotica so Jay went straight up-market on this one and produced a limited edition of 1000 numbered copies, beautifully designed and printed on expensive paper and bound in special cloth that would reflect the character of the book. He didn't want this to fall into the hands of the obvious dirty mac brigade so he priced it accordingly.

Curiously, this had a connection to Jay's past with *Neurotica*, as the man he chose to write the introduction to this bibliography was none other than Legman, the legendary hounder of Jay's principles and editor of the final issue of *Neurotica*. It was appropriate, as Legman was now an established expert on the sexual literature of the 20th century.

It still wasn't a meeting of the minds but money talked louder to Legman those days than it had done in the past, so barring the old reflexive insult, it was a job well done.

The book was a solid triumph with the cognoscenti but left Jay with a sense that maybe he was running out of specific challenges. After all he was not in the publishing business just to make a living and churn out the usual suspects. But where to head to?

With that frame of mind he was open to curious ideas and so found himself becoming a co-publisher and distributor for an original concept. At America's largest book convention he came across Martin and Judy Shepard, who had just created a new imprint, the Second Chance Press with this statement: 'Every year many books are condemned to die, struck down by such diseases as neglect, bad timing or lack of exposure. Quality books are an endangered species. There are special groups for saving everything from whales to historic landmarks. Why not books?'

This was a natural notion for Jay to embrace so without hesitation he signed up. An announcement in the *Bookseller* warned the trade that Landesman was getting serious:

'I want to bring back to the literary mainstream the big ones that got away.'

An initial run of six titles which Jay distributed in Britain met with only modest success and a further ten titles down the line it was apparent that the book-buying public was not interested in literary orphans. It was a disappointment, not least because Jay was a second chance giver to perceived losers on principle, but also because he was getting a bit tired of the rise and fall of his fortunes.

The Shepards went on to become very successful in the States, which perhaps was a sign of the American market's willingness to embrace the underdog concept with greater enthusiasm but it also had a lot to do with the fact that their libraries were flourishing at a time when cut backs in Britain were forcing libraries to make what ever savings they could. There was no budget for orphans.

Jay's Last Stand was to be at the London Book Fair in 1983. 'The Risk that Paid Off' was the headline in the *Bookseller* as it reviewed what would be his last act in publishing:

> The reward for the most eye catching stand at the fair must surely go to that veteran of publishing showmanship, Jay Landesman. It was difficult to tell who was attracting more attention – himself, attired in white linen suit, or the dark beauty looking like a member of a harem, lounging on a chaise-longue, passing out pieces of Turkish Delight on a silver tray surrounded by cardboard eunuchs and leopards – all to promote *The Bedside Book of Erotica*.

There was a lot of action around the stand, all very promising and exciting… but nothing came of it. Jay's style had survived but his substance was no longer viable.

The Don Quixote of Publishing had tilted against his last windmill and he was now, at 65, unhorsed but not unmanned, ready to take on a new challenge.

Bidding farewell to the girls in the sex show next door, he closed shop in Soho and took the remaining stock to the basement of Duncan Terrace where he would retire to live and write his memoirs of a life less ordinary.

'Love is not the dying moan of a distant violin-it's the triumphant twang of the bedspring' (S. J. Perelman)

It now seemed the perfect time for Jay to retrieve the manuscript of the memoirs he had started years earlier. His ancient Smith-Corona wasn't up to the job though, skipping around hesitantly as if reluctant to get the story out. It was time to go onto a word processor and take a fresh look at his early days.

Writing about himself for 8 hours a day, 7 days a week and then talking about it for a couple of hours with his friends and family was not a bad way for Jay to spend his time. I am not saying that most people wouldn't find this the equivalent of going through 'white noise' torture... but for Jay, this was birdsong bliss.

Once finished he sent the manuscript to a leading New York agent, Sterling Lord, who had handled the then unknown Jack Kerouac in the 50s. The months went by and Jay was wondering whether the venerable gentleman had died before doing his duty or whether everyone was on an extended holiday for surely an answer should've arrived before then.

Finally a letter arrived on an autumn morning. It made for uncomfortable reading. Sterling had spent the summer sending the book around. After a series of rejections he reckoned that there were some marketing problems. He was being dismissed with comments like: 'Landesman is a rather obscure figure for American readers and the book would have to be sensationally written in order to have much of a chance' or 'Although Mr Landesman played an interesting role in the Beat period, he doesn't focus enough on it. A book about his publishing life and his friendship with the writers with the intention of giving his special perspective on these people and events could be very worthwhile.'

Ouch.

In London however, he reconnected with Edmund Fisher, once director at Michael Joseph, who was going to start up a new publishing company, and asked him to read the manuscript. He replied after reading it:

> You have written something which has given me more pleasure than any manuscript for a very long time. It is a stimulating piece of compulsive reading... it is honest to a fault, but beyond reasonable expectation. If it isn't honest, not only have you got Fisher fooled, but you could give lessons to Phineas Barnum and David Ogilvy.

But Fisher wasn't Landesman and he went broke before he could get to publish his first book. It ain't as easy as it looks was Jay's rasping line as he sank another Pernod at the French Pub where he got the news. Now that he was no longer 'in bidnez', the martinis and linen suits had been replaced by tinted glasses, a Humphrey Bogart style Burberry and 'artistic' drinking.

These were cruel times for Jay the writer as he waited for his ship to come in. His son Cosmo, who had grown up with a sharp tongue honed by a sharp mind and a deep dislike of his parents publicly lived lives, had written a thinly disguised portrait of Jay in his column in the *Literary Review*, which scholars of patricidal literature would have appreciated:

> I went to see my parents over the weekend. They live in a big rambling house in Hampstead. They are old literary bohemians. Their world stopped in 1968. Some say it was the drugs; others the notices of father's first novel. One critic wrote: 'If the novel is not dead, this one will kill it.' My father was a schizophrenic, alcoholic junkie - but after the reviews he just went to pieces. Father was in the studio, surrounded by his mementoes of a literary life: a letter from Pound begging him not to

visit – Pound feared for his sanity – the stuffed lobster
of Gérard de Nerval, the upper bridgework of Genet
and a signed first edition of Cocteau's shopping list.
Great stacks of yellowing manuscripts grew in every
available inch of space like Triffids of type. The room
was dimly lit so as not to reveal his. tear-stained mas-
cara. Behind a great desk he sat in his. wheelchair, with
hose and plastic bag in one hand, a microphone in the
other. For the past 25 years he had corne to this room
to dictate his memoirs. When I pointed out that the
tape machine had not been plugged in, the shock of 25
years of memoirs down the drain brought an attack of
epilepsy. I left him twitching to visit mother... eventually when I made my escape I looked back at the house.
Through the large french windows I saw two figures
silhouetted by the light: a man slumped in a wheelchair
and a woman in a rage; two of the best minds of a generation destroyed by failure...

Jay felt that his son had portrayed him in the fine Landesman tradition of spoofing satire and was only prepared to quibble over the
description of him in a wheelchair, which he thought would cramp
his style down in the cruel depths of Soho nightlife.

But he needn't have worried. His libido was suitably gratified to
find a charmingly edgy hummingbird at the French Pub, whose love
of champagne and dangerous old men were challenges Jay rose to
magnificently. She became his 27-year-old official mistress. Not bad
for a 66 year old ex-publisher and rejected writer.

Fran, meantime, found herself taking part in a BBC documentary about relationship triangles from a wife's point of view. It was
the old, let's see how we can improve the profile type of decision,
as her market was now shrinking; she couldn't compete with the
high octane younger politicised poets. This was how she began: 'I
didn't have any great expectations of marriage. I have a very happy

marriage. I've been married for thirty five years to a very funny guy and we make each other laugh. I have my unhappy love affairs on the side.'

On being asked why she thought people had affairs:'I know some people think sex is what it is about, but I maintain when you're married a tong time, you get so tired of hearing each other's old stories, those polished gems that you have worked a life time to perfect... When you have an affair, you can trot them out again and they sound fresh and exciting to a new person. I think you'd have to have a tiny shrivelled up heart if there was only place in it for one person for the rest of your life.'

At the end she expressed her confidence that Jay would never abandon her. He happily concurred with those sentiments as did his eminently sensible mistress.

The autumn of 1986 brought welcome news, in the shape of Hope Wurdack (such an American mid-west name), all of four foot eleven and a tender twenty five years old. But it was the badge she wore and the enthusiasm she brought with her that made the young lady the exact tonic Jay and Fran needed.

Her badge read 'theatre producer', the venue: St Louis and the production: a revival of *The Nervous Set*. She arrived at their doorstep and convinced them that she could pull it off with all the panache of a youthful Jay.

The deal was that Jay and Fran would do three nights of cabaret before the show opened. Fran would do her regular act and Jay would read from his memoirs. Hope felt it would be great publicity and help raise money for the production... just the sort of script Jay would encourage. There was also a large fee involved. Juicy.

After 25 years away, Jay and Fran had no idea what to expect from St Louis, but they needn't have worried. It was the return of the prodigal son scenario. A television camera crew interviewed them as they steeped from the plane and the attention never flagged after that. Meeting the cast and having conferences with the director left them little time for play. The two leads had captured them perfectly though it was weird to hear them fighting over issues the two of them still battled over at home.

Fran had the show's musical director to accompany her. Jay was going to read a section from his memoires that dealt with the rise and fall of the Crystal Palace. That was all fine and dandy but what worried Jay was that he couldn't sing and Fran couldn't dance - but that was exactly what they were going to do at the close of the show.

Like all Rip Van Winkle returns, it's difficult to recognise everybody and sometimes to find anybody who might have aged as Jay had. Some had grown up, some simply grown older while others had vanished over the horizon.

But on the first night of the cabaret, his memories of those old St Louis days and nights touched them all. The average age was about Jay's which meant the references and recollections were picked up by one and all with knowing laughter and roundly applauded at the end. Fran's act was received just as impressively. So it was on carpet of confidence that Jay joined Fran in the spotlight and the two of them started dancing to a medley of songs from *The Nervous Set*.

Jay was a past master of the foxtrot and dip, guiding Fran with tender expertise and holding her close. Then, just like in a musical they broke into one of Fran's songs:

> I wasted my whole life
> Messing up yours.
> When I should have been dancing
> I was slamming the doors.
>
> I sulked in the spotlight
> Wearing a frown.
> When I should have been dancing
> I was putting you down

Then Jay sang the middle chorus alone:

We could have been sensational,
A couple of luminous stars,
Could have been inspirational
When all those tomorrows were ours

Then both of them, looking straight into the other's eyes:

I gave you a hard time
Fighting our wars.
When I should have been dancing
I was settling scores.

They stopped dancing. And with their arms around each other they sang to the audience:

When I should have been making sense of my life
I was busy messing up yours.

And then they kissed. To a standing ovation.

The Nervous Set was also well received; in fact it was making Jay feel quite giddy at the prospect of resurrecting his career in St Louis and then setting off for New York with all this creative affection pushing him on and... oops... excuse me... but doesn't this all sound a wee bit familiar... ? It had been almost exactly 30 years ago that Jay had first taken himself off to New York with *The Nervous Set*.

Jay had to remind himself that his life was now in England. He belonged no more to Mid-West America or even to New York America. His habitat was now North London, his hunting ground was Islington arid his home was Duncan Terrace – by the grace of God.

The memories were marvellous but it was time to leave.

When they returned to London they discovered that they were going to become grandparents. Life was moving them both on whether they liked it or not. Fran was more than ready for the role. In fact, so keen that Jay got kind of jealous of this unborn promise.

Jay was not prepared to be so enthusiastic as he knew that this coming event was definitely going to force him to cancel any further subscriptions to the Peter Pan Club. He was already in trouble with the mistress, who began to refer to his forthcoming status as a grandfather and his renewed interest in family matters as though they were approaching signs of senility.

Finally, the day arrived with the birth of the grandson which made Fran feel that 'he was better than a Broadway show' and made Jay nostalgic for his first-born now the father of his grandson, when he was a baby... if you see what I mean.

The mistress finally punched her last clock and headed out into a strange world populated by young people her age.

And Jay. He heard the horns of heaven play as a sudden surge of interest in his book made him sit up straighter.

The book was called *Rebel Without Applause.*

'It's better to be seventy years young than forty years old' (Oliver Wendell Holmes)

The Shepards, who Jay had worked with as a co-publisher of literaryorphans found that his book was hard to put down: We'd like to do your book, Jay. We would consider it a great honour.

Finally Liz Calder of Bloomsbury Press, asked to have a look at the book and decided that she would be prepared to take it on after its publication in the States.

And there he was thinking that he would never feel that adrenaline again.

'What's wrong with having some fun?' says Jay stepping out for a New Day.

The publication of *Rebel Without Applause* came with an intriguing cover quote from Norman Mailer that said: 'Jay and Fran Landesman could be accused of starting it all. By god, were they there at the beginning.'

It emphasised Jay's position as one of the original 'Johnny Appleseed's' of his time, who sowed the cultural landscape with farsighted challenges and alerted the sleepers and feelers to the spectre of the changes to come. John Clellon Holmes was also impressed 'You've done it. You've caught the excitement, the nerves, the aspirations... so much of it eloquent, tough, sad, brave and funny.'

The reviews ran on that theme. Robert Stone, the novelist, said: 'funny and moving, heartening, tragic and outrageous. To read it is to be present at the invention of contemporary America. Of all the published reminiscences of bohemian America in the 50s and 60s, this is the most revealing and the best.'

The Times Educational Supplement saw: 'in America's social and artistic landscape, Jay Landesman's own misfit lifestyle and matrimonial mismatch are absorbing... hilarious.'

The *Irish Post* added: 'Hipsters, jazz musicians, existentialists, comics and actors who reshaped America's social lifestyle can all be found in the pages of *Rebel Without Applause*... this book is both moving and outrageous and definitively a collector's item.'

All well and good and the book did the business, but, Jay was certainly not ready to be a collector's item. Now that he had arrived at the biblical three score and ten, feeling idecently youthful and with all his parts in good working order (as all would agree, but most especially a new mistress that would test that assumption to the limit) it was time to generate a new project.

Much as he loved his children and his grandson, not to mention his 'companion for life', Fran, he was not ready to stand by, offering to dry the dishes, 'cause he didn't have anything better to do...

So it was no surprise that when he got an offer to co-produce a musical version of F. Scott Fitzgerald's *The Great Gatsby*, he jumped at it. After all this was a subject he knew intimately, having patterned his lifestyle on Scott and Zelda for fifty years. He wore the white suits with elegance and wit; remember that he had even changed his name from Irving to Jay.

The offer came from a flamboyant English producer who had had a successful career in Hollywood raising money from big studios for special projects. It was going to be his job to raise the money and get the rights. Everything else would be Jay's responsibility. By now Jay had a powerful address book. It wasn't a book of spells that could make things happen at will but he did know how to get hold of people and that was all he needed give Jay an ear and he would have you over for dinner and involved quicker than you could say... No way Jay.

In no time at all Jay got his side of the bargain up and hoping. Simon Callow faxed his acceptance as director. Richard Rodney Bennet for the music. Jeremy Brooks for the book and Fran for the lyrics. Callow suggested Keith Carradine would be perfect as Jay Gatsby.

The tingle of anticipation was on again. But who was going to let the side down? Would everyone play their parts correctly this time and answer the bell when it rang?

The first hint that the dawn of a new age for Jay, a hit not a miss, might have to be put on hold was when he discovered that his co-producer had set up office, so to speak, at the Picasso coffee shop on the King's Road, home to legendary has-beens and big league bull shitters, in his attempts to hunt down a big money man.

If only t was that easy. An American was found and charmed as he claimed to have recently come into a large inheritance. Jay probably knew better but let expectation get in the way of a reality check and his producer, Peter Cranwell, high on too many cappuccinos, forgot to do a bullshit test. The guy was a fake.

But worse than that was the problem Cranwell was having trying to get the rights from the Fitzgerald estate. Ironically for Jay, the man who could have made the difference to him when he took' *The Nervous Set* to New York all those years ago (30 years earlier) but who never got there in time, the still powerful old boy from St Louis, the producer David Merrick, was contesting the film rights.

In the mean time Jay decided to take on all the producing responsibilities, getting rid of Cranwell, and trying to raise the money himself. All the original participants had by now bowed out as promises got to their sell-by-date and nothing had happened. Back to the address book and back at bat.

Lord Sainsbury was indeed a great fan but 'no, he wouldn't be an investor'.

Jay's nephew, Rocco Landesman, son of his brother Fred, who had become one of Broadway's most daring producers of controversial plays, also said: 'It would be difficult to raise the money necessary when looking at the record of two flop films of Gatsby. Best to leave it as a novel.'

Undaunted, Jay tried the big West End producers Cameron Mackintosh, Trevor Nunn, Bill Kenwright and Lloyd Webber but found that they too could not see the light in that tunnel.

But all was not lost. A new composer with connections at Time Warner was found. Working with Fran, Jason McAuliffe came up with such a wonderful score that TW offered their platform theatre in New York for a full cast performance. It was going to cost very little as the project was being subsidised by McAuliffe's enthusiasm. Producers and potential backers would be invited to the performance.

Jay and Fran drank a toast to their renewed hopes of finding their niche on The Great White Way and flew to New York.

It was as exciting as any first night they had shared. The cast turned in an inspiring performance. The audience was enthusiastic. The songs were on the button and the lyrics went straight to the heart. But.Again the producers failed to see it as a Broadway winner. They all loved it. But lovely doesn't put bums on seats and sentiment doesn't make anyone richer. They left with their hands in their pockets.

Jay was an old hand at these disappointments by now so he had enjoyed the parties leading up to that night knowing that he wouldn't want to hang around if his baby got strangled at birth again.

If New York was the cathedral of dreams, Broadway was the high altar, and its producers the priests of its passion. Jay and Fran were simply one of thousands of devotees that flocked there in the hope that their offerings would be accepted. It was not to be.

'How can I tell what I think till I see what I say?' (E. M. Forster)

Jay's second book of memoirs came out. Again with a fun title: *Jay-walking*. It fared well with the press, receiving some favourable reviews. But while *Rebel* had dealt with a time and a place that was far away and exotic for its English readers, this book dealt with the swinging scene in London all the way to the end of the Thatcher years. This was familiar territory for anyone interested in the cultural tapestry of the time. Hundreds of books had been published and millions of words written about these times, so Jay's contribution was considered just another handful of sand on that particular beach. Fine sand that it was, it was still a hell of a big beach.

Jay was a liberated man of seventy three, almost free of his fear that he would go to his grave an anonymous and forgotten man. Now he could concentrate on the frivolous side of his nature..

An appearance on the *Antiques Roadshow* where one of the paintings in his home was assessed at £50,000 to his utter consternation, proved to be a big hit with viewers and his local market stallholders giving him for awhile a notoriety that extended all the way down from Islington to Soho. He enjoyed that.

After all Soho was a home away from home for the man. Dean Street was his road with its four drinking and entertainment stations conveniently situated within walking distance from each other.

The Colony Room was one of the original drinking clubs in Soho, dating back to the days when pub timetables provided less drinking time than artists and decadent aristos of the street needed to remedy the ills of the world, flee from domestic arrangements or contemplate a life of alcohol fuelled passion. Drinking, talking and screwing were the pleasures on the menu. Jay had found the Colony at an early stage after arriving in London and remained a regular though not devout member of its inner circle. The devotees after all, died long before he had any intention of doing so.

The Groucho Club was next down the street. Set up in the 1980s, it was a home for the more successful members of the arts and entertainment guide to London. It was a club to do business in as well as providing a stage for ageing dilettantes and aspiring networkers. Jay was a founder member there and responsible for keeping the bartenders sharp on their Martini skills. It was also an office for his meetings and a salon for his conquests.

The French Pub was an old fashioned watering hole that ministered to the needs of those who were finding their artistic and writing legs, those were losing their legs but had made their contribution and the ones who occasionally had something to say but were basically legless most of the time.

The last station on the road was Jerry's, where you went to when the bell struck eleven and midnight was approaching. A club for theatre folk but also for those who could bring some passion to the early hours of the morning. Membership was not always required but Jay was an honorary one anyway.

His forays mixed the need for stimulating conversation with buddies and strangers alike and the teasing necessary to get the ladies interested. Girls and ladies were surprisingly susceptible to his dry wit and easygoing manner - perhaps because of his legendary largesse at the bar - or because he still cut a fine figure for a man of his age, always witha dapper and ageless sense of cool embodied in his Panama hat, white linen suit and technicolour tie.

Fran understood his appetite for new challenges and encouraged him to bring her back the best tidbits of gossip from the streets of Soho. Freedom of choice had, after all, been at the epicenter of their time together and they could even joke that the most outrageous thing the two of them could do, would be to get a divorce. That was said with a Cheshire cat smile and a lopsided St Louis grin.

In any case, Fran's career was in one of its cyclical periods of resurgence. In 1994 she had a mini-musical called *Invade My Privacy,* chosen for a charity performance at the Criterion Theatre. The *New Yorker's* drama critic, John Lahr, saw the show and thought it had potential to go to New York… but changes were required that proved in the end a hurdle that couldn't be cleared to everybody's satisfaction. But nevertheless it brought Fran back to the public eye and the reassuring pleasures of performing – what Jay would call the 'Doctor Footlights' syndrome because it would clear up any symptoms of ghostly illnesses that might be lurking.

Jay was now comfortable basking in whatever success Fran brought to the Landesman beach while he made himself busy making sandcastles at the edge of the timeless sea.

Our man was now approaching his eightieth birthday, just a year short of the millennium, and he still hadn't worked out what was left of his future. Of course it still involved a determined attempt to re-work his career and he enjoyed being mentioned by Alistair Cook in one of his *Letters from America*, as one of two people whom (the other was Anthony Burgess), he had met on a visit to London '… the old incorrigible Beatnik Jay Landesman… who now deplores that the youth of today were imitating that destructive and self-destructive business of undermining the traditional values of American society in the name of self-expresion and freedom.'

Hard to say whether that was said with a straight face. Maybe it was another way of liberating his life from any sort of predictability. The fear of routine had always ruled his life; if he felt the dulling of the moment the first suspect would always be that dirty rat.

'Haven't I seen you around before?' he would growl at the face or the motion, the feeling or the notion of this familiarity.

He thought this might have something to do with his mother, the lady who wanted him to be a serious citizen… like a dentist – and why not. She died disappointed in him, a fate he shared with more than quite a few sons of mothers that will always know what is best for their children, no matter what age they are.

The truth is that Jay was lucky to have had a mother who gave him the freedom to rebel and someone strong to rebel against; that she also gave him love for the money to go along with his soul of a chancer was just blind luck.

Jay's health had held up well over the years. A man who avoided stress by enjoying the fruits of a leisurely stroll through life as well as a sympathetic and balanced approach to its pleasures and vices, had never needed sport or exercise to keep his doctor's happy. But in 1998 he suffered the first of a series of angina attacks. He blamed them on the fact that his heart was no longer hunting and had too much time on its hands, so got bored and restless. But his father and brother died following strokes so he let himself get checked over.

The result was that he was put in a ward full of bypass-scarred veterans that made him the novice at this game. He turned it into a resident Landesman show with a comforting trail of visitors queuing up to see him and reassure him that they were keen to have him back. His cardiac specialist turned out to be a closet poet with a penchant for the epic poem. Par for the course really... Jay always found the real dreamer however well they otherwise disguised themselves as serious punters of the professional world.

The operation went well. He was not yet required for celestial duties and his mortal coil was still his to keep and look after.

It did make him want to take stock and lay out an inventory of his various lives and inventions. What was clear was that his marriage to Fran was the only aspect he had taken seriously white trying to find the best way to enjoy life and the contradictions in his own character. He acknowledged that he had been too restless and inquisitive to ever have been able to build anything of lasting significance beyond the encouragement he had always given those who needed help in taking off or adjusting their masks. He suspected that he was a nice Jewish boy at heart, with a radical notion of sex behind a lot of his projects to entertain and give pleasure to people - hey we all need an engine to get us going down the road.

Curiosity may have killed the cat but it proved to be Jay's ally throughout his life. Not only for his use but also for those who wondered:

'Who was that man that just walked into my life?...
'They call him Jay...'
'You don't say....'
'Keep him away from me.'

Just kidding. Generally speaking it was quite the opposite.

'Some folk want their luck buttered.'
(Thomas Hardy)

In his 80th year Jay decided to take a shot at getting his story up on the silver screen. A natural ambition for a man who had already laid out the bones of his lifestyle and the lifeblood of his dreams in every conceivable public forum. From using it as material for his abortive stand up comedian act in the early days of the Crystal Palace to his play, the musical, books of memoires, appearing in his wife's poetry plus all the bars and gin joints that he had walked into.

Like most of his projects, this one originated in a drinking den, The French Pub on this occasion. Over a lip-smackingly good martini, he found himself talking to a film producer about the art of sending scripts to producers as he had finished collaborating on one that was based on *The Nervous Set*. Things moved on after a second martini and soon he was promising to send a copy to his drinking companion, Aubrey Weller.

Jay could feel the rise and rise of unrealistic expectations, but he reckoned his heart was up to it so he got in touch with an old sparring partner from his Crystal Palace days who used to book acts for him in New York, Irvin Arthur. The man had gone through his own ups and downs but had landed on his feet in Hollywood as one of the agents for Jim Carrey, making him a handshaker of the movers in that town. He promised to read the script, intrigued by the vision of old times in New York being revisited. But he did warn Jay that he was a slow reader

Jay was already debating whether he would allow Jim Carrey to play him. His morning walks with Fran to their favourite café for breakfast had become exercises in skipping and smiling a lot.

While waiting, always the waiting, for the results of his initial promotion of the film, Jay and his screenwriter Terence Doyle got invited to go to the Cannes Film Festival by a London production company which had also been charmed by the script, Media Circus.

Interviews were set up on their own yacht with major and minor networks to promote the Jay Landesman story in the flesh. Jay decided that if this would have to be his life after the film was made... he could deal with it. It was a dangerously high level of attention for this eighty year old, but hey, somebody's got to do it. He capped his performance with a practical lecture at the bar on how to make the perfect martini. A half page photograph adorned the festival's main magazine the following day.

That would be Jay's high water mark on the project as progress went into a holding pattern... and time would go by as it has to, with the script travelling to different parts of the world and into a variety of hands as contacts were made and interest expressed. But the world of film has got more barracudas than the Amazon river, more sharks than an Australian coast line, more fantasists than a fairy tale and more sons of bitches than an American jail. The Jihad for Silver Screen Fame puts Sodom and Gornorrah to shame.

How many years does it take for a slow reader to finish reading a script?

How many lies are disguised in a show of admiration? The truth is that between Jay's optimism and his script writer's belief in his work and their tireless struggle to give life to their baby, lay the unbridgeable gap of a Hollywood egg they could not fertilise.

Jay's address book had run out of power and all he had left was a sympathy vote from family and friends which wouldn't get him a power seat at his local diner.

But he did have the secret admiration of the younger entertainment hustlers and new pioneers down Dean Street way, who saw him as a model of never- say- die spirit, encouraging them to keep pushing at the doors of indifference until their talents got the recognition they needed. To keep driving that ambition and race it up and down Hope Street until the right person threw open their window and shouted out their name.

Jay now had some health issues to deal with. A bladder problem was diagnosed as a cancer. A great fear came into the Landesman world. Was the millennium going to be reached or was he going to fall just short of it?

The fates decided that the man had the right to see his own way into the 21st century. The cancer decided that it was wasting its time and was treated successfully. Jay decided to get more comfortable with his age and begin cleaning up his act.

For a start it was clear that Fran was still attracting interest wherever clever rhyme and pithy insight was appreciated, whether it was the poetry or the cabaret circuit. The cognoscenti asked him how he felt about her receiving so much attention. His reply was: - It hasn't reached danger point until they start referring to me as Mr Fran Landesman.'

There had been a time, when he was still a light dancing seventy year old, he had said that he wanted to grow old disgracefully. But he decided he had changed his mind. He now saw it as the last interesting challenge. He felt no need to reappraise either critics or friends, nor did he feel he had to do anymore cultivating of his talents or desires. He believed that longevity was his best ally and would see him through to his proper place in the scheme of things. He was reminded of Hubie Blake, who made it with his songs when he hit 90 and said: 'If I had known I was going to be so successful I'd have taken better care of myself!'

*'I got everything I wanted / It was more
than I expected / It wasn't enough' (Fran L.)*

How do you find the path to the fields of your past when you find
that the seeds you planted and left behind have been turned into a
garden where you are not recognised?

Jay felt that much of what had happened to the 20th century social and cultural environment was in some measure due to the fact
that he was one of the brave few to peel back the top of Pandora's
box after it had been hidden by the events leading up to and following the Second World War.

If you have forgotten what I mean then go back to the beginning
of this tale and refresh yourself. If you still can't figure it out then go
figure why you are reading this chronicle in the first place!

In the spirit of leaving celebrity lusts behind and celebrating life
for living, Jay made a conscious effort to stop plugging either his
past or his sense of himself as a product. As he said: 'It was a relief
to find that people have learnt how to promote themselves and are
doing a good job at it. I don't need to do anything but nod at their
ideas when in the past I had to take them shopping for them.'

Now Jay isn't the sort of person who pays any mind to those who
like to believe that things work by serendipity and magical asso-
ciations. Yet I believe that in a subconscious way he has made that
connection. He found himself a beneficiary, and a substantial one
at that, of the will of a fella who had once been his ticket collector
at the door of the Crystal Palace. Along the way he had made some
serious money. He had been a serious pigeon fancier and Jay had,
without much thought about it, given him to believe that he also
had a soft spot for these creatures. For over 40 years Jay had kept in
touch with him always asking after the pigeons in a whimsical sort
of way, but in truth having little real affection for them.

Then he found himself with this yearly stipend that made a pleasant difference to his lifestyle and would you know it, he starts communing with the pigeons in the park by Duncan Square. The day a white pigeon flew over to him and landed on his outstretched hand when he called to it, tickled him no end. The fact that he happened to have some crumbs of bread in his hand was of no consequence. He had bonded. Not something to tell the ladies in the Groucho about, but a soft thought to share with Fran.

They shared these things now like once they had shared the peccadillos of a spicy life. Hot chilli stories of naughty nights had become hot cross bun tales at noon.

Jay and Fran's 50th anniversary.

'Memories are hunting horns, whose sound dies on the wind' (G. Apollinaire)

The young man from St Louis is now an old boy in London. They both had a dream: one to rebel and the other to be remembered.

The 21st century had arrived and left the legacy of one Irving 'Jay' Landesman receding into the thickening mists of the 20th. He was now in his early eighties and spending more time with the surviving locals of the neighbourhood who were pals from yesteryear. That is a feast of diminishing returns of course as the bells tolls regularly for the death train to take another away from home and hearth.

Jay and Fran went on their morning walks to Al's, their coffee shop for many years. Every morning the routine would not vary. He would wait by the front door. She came down from her bedroom den which had been her private space for decade; he came up from his basement den that had been his busy terminal for years. He offered his arm, she took it, and off down the road they went with her telling him what new inspiration she had and he telling her the news of the day.

They were closer than ever despite the fact that they had long since moved from separate beds, to separate rooms and separate quarters, separate social events and separate lunches. Especially lunches. As Fran said:' I married you for better or worse, but not for lunch.'

One morning, over a steaming and satisfying cup of coffee, Fran said that it was time for the two of them to 'wrap it up'. She also had another way of putting it: 'Waiter, the check!'

They had thought of a hand-in-hand departure in the back of the Bentley with a last martini as the hose from the exhaust filled the car with finality. Jay was still a romantic seventy year old when they mooted that one and Fran was in one of her poetic blue moods like 'L is for Lost'.

Whatever. Jay had lost his passion for that scenario, particularly when his body started to rebel on him and sent him sliding to the precipice of his own mortality. Suicide may have seemed like a painless option but he was not prepared to do dead yet.

In fact he joined a health club. Probably as a place to practice his wit and wisdom on the weight trainers, but he was also looking to keep his shrinking frame from losing its strength. He was still driving his car, getting on and off buses into Soho and holding nanas with the fair barmaids at the French Pub and the wrists of the waitresses at the Groucho Club. Oh yes, he still needed his strength all right.

Fran s health was not good either, not least because she had spent most of her time lying in bed, writing, being visited, watching television, eating and generally using it as the nerve centre of her life's operations. The doctor told her she had to do some exercise. People had been telling her that for years but she acted as if she hadn't ever heard that before.

So she said to Jay: 'Jaybird? Maybe I should join your health club. It's right across the street. No matter what I say, drag me by the hair into that club.'

Jay felt proud that his fifty years of character building had not been in vain. His muscles were also doing him proud and Fran's aches and pains gradually disappeared. Unfortunately so did the health club. That part of Islington was clearly not a place for the health conscious.

Will you still need me, will you still feed me... when I'm 84?

Jay realised that he had made his last trip to New York in the year 2003. He hadn't been well (he needed a pace maker put in for a heart that was ticking at a different beat to the one the rest of his body was happy with) and really shouldn't have flown but it was one way to reassure the world and his friends that he really was alive if not kicking. Not fly to New York when there was a creative agenda on the menu. You gotta be kidding. It had been a trip to get Fran's show, *Sin City Fables*, sorted out in an off-Broadway venue and keep up her contacts with her music publishers and encourage a new generation to find their way to her songs.

But his agenda had been limited. No Broadway shows or night clubbing, no movies or museums, no girls to flirt with or friends to visit – they were dead or dying. What he realised is that it took a lot of energy to get around New York and to track things down. Unlike his London town, which was as familiar and tasty as the old Stage's pastrami sandwich which he had fallen in love with when he had first arrived in New York those 55 years earlier. The truth was the new pastrami was not to his taste. Things happen.

He may have been an 84 year old going on 65 and the libido of a spotty teenager but the truth was that he could just about get to the batting plate these days. The last heart scare had put paid to the locomotion section of his brain, (no funny remarks here), that prevented him from walking properly. In fact it made it unlikely the man would get on the dance floor again or get laid, unless it was orchestrated by pros. Nothing wrong with that you might say, but he always preferred the company of gifted amateurs.

It did give him the chance' to walk around with a well decorated and historic cane, from which he hung a compass that told him, so he said, how to steer clear of the bull shifters now that he couldn't speed away from them anymore.

He felt lucky that he was living with a wife, okay she was two floors away from him, who smiled as she said when he complained of his disability: 'They shoot horses don't they?'

In fact he knew he was lucky when he counted it up. They didn't like the same films, friends, fashion or fiction but they did like each other's looks and spirit. They seldom argued about money or morals, manners or mistresses. They both wished they could sing better. Neither of them did 'marches', but they enjoyed walking together and holding hands. They respected each other's space, knocking on each other's doors before walking in. They liked to sleep alone but they enjoyed unexpected kisses.

They both liked to perform in public, though only one of them was prepared to do it for free. They both accused the other of being egomaniacal but were sympathetic to the other's ageing. They both think they had a smashing time as it happens and loved their children too.

'Getting Forgetful' (Fran Landesman)

They could now laugh at their pursuit of success as if hadn't domi-
nated so much of their life. Jay admits that: '..we never cracked the
big time but we had a lot of chances. Maybe we didn't find the perfect way to live but we sure gave it a try. We're still trying. As you get
older, it's easier… and if you are lucky you find the simple things are
often the most successful.'

Fran would be able to write these lines in her poem to remind Jay
of where they were:

> I'm getting forgetful.
> The names and the faces I used to adore
> Now slip from my memory.
> No wonder they don't come around anymore…
>
> I'm getting forgetful.
> Old movies and novels all seem brand new
> Like I've never met them.
> The one thing I haven't forgotten is you.
> Although I'm forgetful
> I haven't forgotten you.

The Landesman family had been rehearsing their act for years
round the kitchen table. There was Jay and Fran, their oldest son
Cosmo, the writer and film critic, and Miles the musician who
would nod in time to the wordsmiths beating out their line. The
subject matter was always incendiary as opinions were strongly held
and contentious. Whether it was about the parties and the flirting,
the frustrations and successes, the feuds and reappraisals, the love

affairs and the gossip, the rights and the wrongs, the poetry and the songs, the banal and the unique.

It was Fran's laboratory for exploratory verbal research and it was Jay's litmus for the birth and still-birth of his working ideas.

Guests were not allowed to take themselves too seriously but were invited to contribute wittily and with conviction to the rapid fire exchanges of a family who used words with the ease of a sea gull catching fish.

It was also the place that gave their two children the filter and the challenge to find their own terms with which to deal with the world outside. Miles was a cool cat with a defiantly minimalist take on the responsibilities of being a good citizen. He had a good heart and played a good guitar, but was distracted by the pleasures of being a rascal, enjoying the raunchy side of life and his music reflected that. The lad seemed to have an instinctive understanding of his parents life style with no desire to challenge it or be bothered by it, anticipating no more of a traditional life than Jay and Fran had. He had a simple respect for what anyone was doing with their lives, comfortable with all the range of visitors that passed through the Landesman front door, be they tradesmen or masters of their trade.

Cosmo on the other hand, had a different take on events. He was the oldest son, Jay Jr., but in reality very different from his father. He was a sharp and observant kid, opinionated too, surrounded by his parent's friends and listening to the games people played and the words they used. But when he arrived in England he went from being an All American boy to a stranger in a strange land, having to find himself an English character to inhabit so that he wouldn't stand out. Unlike his father, who Cosmo said '...boomed across Britain, larger than life in a society that was still repressed and reticent. Jay was vibrant, the terminator of uptightness.'

He was much less comfortable than Miles, about the public agenda of his parents. In fact, as he saw it '...while we were growing up, Jay and Fran were going back to adolescence... we were bringing up the parents.'

They were never Mum and Dad, but Jay and Fran... 'like Simon and Garfunkel or Scott and Zelda Fitzgerald.'

Cosmo's rebellion, if you could call it that, was to become the conservative arm of the Landesman fraternity. Admiring and respecting his parents successes but not approving of their life styles. He joined Jay's publishing company, but as all eldest sons must do, eventually set off onto his own intellectual journey which led him into a career in journalism and his own writing. Their paths would clash for many years after that, with Jay's extrovert showmanship at odds with Cosmo's desire for a lower profile of artistic and introspective endeavour.

But in the end there would be tolerance, if not always understanding The thing is that as one gets older one doesn't have to and maybe doesn't want to ask so many questions. The result is not ignorance, particularly if one has already had a curiosity filled life, but a mature acceptance that the past can never save the present, and the present is what gives us our future.

Jay and Fran had tolerated each other's lifestyle because it had been settled upon with an honesty that was very rare in their generation. Only now, in the last decade of the 20th century and in these early years of the 21st, have people tried to arrive at this honesty through the countless self help books and counselling programmes that exist to lead the truth teller through the minefield which is the landscape of deception.

Before the book comes the word, before the writer comes the doer, before the people comes the pioneer.

Jay always told Fran that he was no damn good as an old fashioned faithful man. She was impressed enough with his honesty that she wrote a lyric about it:

> Don't fall in love with me.
> It wouldn't do.
> I couldn't ever be
> Faithful to you.

Don't fall in love with me.
I'm no damn good.
You'd only lose your way
In my neighbourhood.

I'm not your destiny.
Kiss me and run.
Don't fall in love with me.
Don't spoil the fun.

Jay was a man of paradoxes which perhaps only a poet like Fran would have been able to unravel without destroying the man-made fibres of their relationship. He wanted to sip at the lip of many a pretty dame but also wanted to stay married to the same woman. His mistresses knew it and his sons did too.

He had been an embarrassment to his sons from the first day they had had to go to school, with him attached to them like an eccentric creature come alive from a grown up comic book. What did he care that they felt mortified by his vintage Bentley and innovative street gear. He wasn't going to dress down to be there on parent's day for Christ's sake

But Fran says he was a good father. A loving and caring father. But a hugely mortifying father with far too many quirks for youngsters and teenagers who don't want their parents to discuss their sex lives in public or their dirty laundry on the stage. Not hard to understand. Jay never fully fathomed this until his son Cosmo discovered the power of a waspish tongue and a mighty pen.

Jay poked fun at the intelligentsia but wanted credit for his originality from the historians of 20th century culture. He had despised the insular thinkers who hunkered down in their intellectual trenches and never went out into the firing line to deal with the grey establishment hordes in hand to mouth battle. Yet he wanted them to recognise that without his efforts and those like him they would have been no more better than bunker boys.

But the mad dogs of the front line are always forgotten in the time of peace...

He hated show-offs and grandstanders and players who pissed on your shoes to show you how tough they are, but he spent most of his life waving at a gallery even as he was unable to hit that home run and was getting caught on the bases.

Show me the inner sanctum and I will show you a most unattractive breed of men who thought themselves above all others and without compare. But Jay was most interested indeed in the secrets of that sanctum. St Louis was a terribly bigoted city. Jews were not excepted from exclusion. The Catholic community controlled all access to the best clubs and memberships to the most elite inner circles.

So Jay satirised them and challenged them but always entertained them because he wasn't asking them to change... which they loved of course... much as royalty loves and needs its jesters, though it goes without saying they must have the royal seal of approval. Once anointed by the movers and shakers, he enjoyed his time with the doublebarrelled aristocracy of the city. He flirted with the swells and the ladies of the oldest families, with a rollicking panache that made them feel dangerously seduced and charmingly flattered.

Don't forget the temptation that came from Henry Luce, when he offered to buy into *Neurotica* to make it a stable mate of *Time* and *Life* magazines. Jay was just a farthing away from selling his soul for a dream of cucumber sandwiches in Connecticut with the cream of literary New York.

What saved him then and would continue to be his lifeboat throughout all the stormy weather he encountered as captain of the good ship *Landesmania* was the steady and yet also not so steady, ready and yet ready to leave presence of his sworn companion Fran. He loved her in a way that was not easy to understand for those standing outside.. and even from the inside it sometimes was tough:

Will you stay by my side
Or love me and run?
Are we playing for keeps
Or just having fun?

Fran remembered Jay in many of her lyrics and poems. He and
his life, lived for the fun of it, were an inspiration. She remembers a
sleek and graceful man who was a great dancer with a salty sense of
humour and funny one-liners. When others would complain about
a hard day after a late night's carousing he would give his wry smile
and crack 'I'm afraid I've got a small day tomorrow.'

The man brought the sweet taste of fun into a depressive and melancholic girl's life, but then had to learn that that this was never going
to be exclusively for her. This sent her to find her writing comforts
which became her talent and in time her poems would be providing
the bittersweet truths of love and trials of life to the world at large...
who loved her for it...much as she loved Jay... as Jay loved her.

Yet she acknowledged that while she had more patience than him
when it came to work, he was the one who could make a social occasion work. As often as not she would arrive a party with Jay and
after a few minutes, getting ready to duck out, whispering to Jay:

'Too many adults here. Gotta scram.'

He. on the other hand, timed his departures to coincide with
the tides of sexual possibilities and stimulating opportunities.
What more could he ask for? And for 60 years he rarely pushed
his luck beyond the waterline. He was a master timer and left many
a peender with a sense that they had over stayed their welcome as
soon as he had gone.

But there was no question that between the highs and the low
blows, was a place that belonged just to them, lit by their very own
Landesman Chandeliers, with Crystal Palace mirrors and *Nervous*
memories...

You will always be my friend,
In spite of time,

Landesmania!

Laughing at the latest trend,
In spite of time.

Epilogue

Jay has got his financial affairs in shape and his life in working order. There is a spirit of reconciliation afoot in the Landesman household as the past is put to pasture and the old ghosts are silenced.

This story is concluding in the month of February of the year 2004. Jay will be 85 this year and reckons that the heavenly bean counters have another few years for him. There is life to be lived, martinis to be enjoyed and misfits to have fun with.

Who knows – there may yet be another project lurking in the depths of the good vessel, but it is time for me to get off and wave goodbye as she sails on.

All seem well who sail on the good ship *Landesmania*.

Index

Index

TIGER OF THE STRIPE

Typeset by Tiger of the Stripe

in Adobe Jenson Pro,

an OpenType fount,

using Adobe InDesign CS

on a Macintosh running

Mac OS X Panther

www.ingramcontent.com/pod-product-compliance
Lightning Source LLC
Chambersburg PA
CBHW060421100426
42812CB00030B/3263/J